CRITICAL PRAISE FOR FLETCHER RHODEN'S WORK

for REDHEAD CUBAN HAUSFRAU HUSBAND The Musical, written & directed by Fletcher Rhoden, music & lyrics by Fletcher Rhoden

From EsterBoldberg's Views From A Blog

Another fabulous night of theater in Los Angeles!

From Rich Borowy's Theater Blog

by Rich Borowy The world premier of Fletcher Rhoden's REDHEAD CUBAN HAUSFRAU HUSBAND, a saga that takes a backstage look at television's first comedy couple and the sitcom that made them famous.

Joan Elizabeth Kennedy is the Redhead, Derek Rubiano is the Cuban, and Jodi Skeris and Michael-Anthony Nozzi are the Hausfrau and the Husband. When the concept of television was in its salad days, one of the most popular sitcoms of that era featured a wacky housewife married to a Cuban bandleader, while her neighbors played a supporting role; the wife was the redhead's "partner in crime", and the husband was just a friendly ally.

Off stage and off camera, these four were a different bunch. They bickered with one another, sometimes each one would upstage the next, and the Redhead nearly got in hot water with the

Commie crashers (lead by none other than J. Edgar himself) because of some minor and rather innocent act she did some twenty years before. In spite of all of these antics, each player did their part providing millions with plenty of laughs that still exist to this very day!

If the above premise sounds an awful like a well known comedian, another well known Latin bandleader, while the supporting cast appears to be a pair of character performers of the 1950s, let's do a little 'splainin' around here! Sure, this storyline uses facts that peppered up with enough creative license, but playwright Fletcher Rhoden didn't (or couldn't) obtain a license to use the actual names of this foursome! That's OK though!

What makes up for a collection of nameless characters is the musical score composed by the same writer! (Guess what? He also directs this show, too--as well as operating the lighting and sound!) The songs hold a lot of wit and inspiration. Some of the score is based on a classic vaudeville type rendition, while the other tunes in the repertory showcases the rich details of an on-again off-again relationship that made this couple what they became to be, while their business side added to their conflict. Michael-Anthony Nozzi adds the choreography (assisted by Derek Rubiano) to this production that works well for the intimate stage this cast has to deal with.

This reviewer will add one element to this production that seems very fitting. Unlike traditional 99 seat-type theaters that exist around the Los Angeles area, this stage piece is performed within the lower level of Mt. Hollywood Congregational Church. The building itself dates back to 1915 making this structure historical to its neighborhood. So when one arrives, one may witness a setup consisting of an assortment of plastic lawn chairs (with a few royal blue Knoll office chairs placed within the first row), nestled semi-circle in front of a small narrow stage. Even though one is not attending a stage show in a palace, that is not the reason why one even patronizes a live show! (Who really goes to the theatre just for the theater itself?) But one will definitely become entertained with what takes place on the stage, rather than for the stage!

REDHEAD CUBAN HAUSFRAU HUSBAND is a tribute to the people behind all of the laughter that's been going on for over a half century! Sometimes the Redhead, et. al, may not have been laughing, but that is why everyone loves 'em! Or as the Redhead would exclaim, "Weeeeellll......."

For LAST TANGO WITH MARLON, a novella by Fletcher Rhoden (Trafford, 2008)

5.0 out of 5 stars A unique and entertaining story, well worth the read, December 6, 2008
By Midwest Book Review
What conversations does one of the most legendary Hollywood stars have with his best friend? "Last Tango with Marlon" is a novella version of Fletcher Rhoden's critically acclaimed two-act

play following the relationship of an over-the-hill Marlon Brando and his best friend Wally Cox. A unique and entertaining story, "Last Tango with Marlon" is well worth the read.

Review from BookPleasures.com

by Gary Dale Cearley

Bravissimo! I swear this was one enjoyable read!

Fletcher Rhoden's Last Tango with Marlon was entertaining and enlightening. When I read this book I not only felt that Fletcher knew these two men but that he knew them well.

The book opens with Marlon on the telephone trying to make arrangements to star in a film about the Dee Brown classic Bury my Heart at Wounded Knee. It is at this point where he first evokes the ghost of his childhood friend, fellow actor, Wally Cox.

The entire novella is a dialogue between Wally Cox and Marlon Brando about their highs and lows, their triumphs and defeats. I can certainly tell that the background research on both men was lengthy and thorough. The dialogue throughout is exceptionally believable. I didn't know much about Wally Cox before but after reading the book I found some clips of him on YouTube and could see that character in Rhoden's Last Tango with Marlon was indeed a true to life portrayal. Wally Cox was just as I imagined him to be.

And the character for Marlon Brando was very telling as well.

With Wally he wore his short comings on his sleeve and Wally obliged the same. We learn at least what we imagine to be their deepest secrets and was also learned of their long standing regard for one another. And though Wally is just a ghost, like in the Dickens tale, he leaves Marlon Brando with the message that as bad as Brando may have mucked up his life, especially with his children, he can still change. The ball is in his court....

How true!

This short book is amazingly well written and henceforth I will read anything of Fletcher Rhoden's that I get a chance to.

for LAST TANGO WITH MARLON, a play in two acts (Fletcher Rhoden.com, 2008)

Review from What's Up magazine

by Willard Manus, Aug. 2008

Marlon Brando and Wally Cox were boyhood friends back in Evanston, Illinois. They remained close for the rest of their lives, most of which were spent in Hollywood, where Brando became rich and famous for his film work, Cox somewhat less so for his TV accomplishments (Mr. Peepers, Hollywood Squares). Their intense and revealing relationship was the subject of a recent stage play, Last Tango With Marlon, which was done in L.A. in this year. Written and directed by Fletcher Rhoden with Frank Cavestani starring as Brando, Raf Mauro as Cox, the hour-long drama is set in 1974. Brando's flagging career has been revitalized by his startling performances in The Godfather and Last Tango In Paris, but these triumphs haven't served to slay the actor's personal demons. Deeply unhappy, drinking to excess, on the verge of a nervous breakdown, Brando summons up the ghost of his recently deceased friend Cox, who then proceeds to try and save Brando from self-destructing. Alternately lecturing, then babying Brando, Cox begins to bring his friend around. They share memories of their unhappy childhoods (parental abuse and disapproval), their struggles in show business. Soon the two of them are joking and clowning around, performing favorite song and dance routines, investigating the highs and lows of their personal lives. Mauro and Cavestani are a marvelous team; each brings his character to life with flair and fire, capturing the many sides of Brando and Cox with impressive skill. Working together effortlessly, like an old vaudeville team, they make Last Tango With Marlon a theatrical dance to remember.

Review from The Tolucan Times:

Last Tango With Marlon Explores the Friendship Between Brando and Cox
By Beth Temkin on February 06, 2008

Fletcher Rhoden has written a fascinating play about the unlikely friendship between Wally Cox and Marlon Brando, and it's fast-moving and full of interesting tidbits.

Veteran actors Frank Cavestani as Marlon, and Raf Mauro as Wally, resemble only slightly their famous counterparts, but they make it work. There's Frank as a heavy Marlon, complete with his familiar high-pitched and halting delivery, and then there's Raf, as the short, bespectacled Wally, who is intensely comedic. Marlon, aware of his being fat, and distanced from Tahiti, his children, and good roles, is not in the best frame of mind, but is happier when Wally comes back from the dead after one year. The play opens with Marlon talking to Wally's ashes.

Rhoden's meticulous research gives the audience insight into their relationship. They knew each other from childhood on, both of their mothers were drunks, and Marlon's father was cruel and abusive. Beyond the family connection, they were connected both intellectually and emotionally. During the 1 1/2 hour play, they match wits and act out a few scenes from Marlon's movies, such as Viva Zapata, taking on different accents for whomever they're portraying, and The Last Tango in Paris, where Marlon felt uncomfortably exposed. In fact, Marlon wanted to be a comedian like Wally, who shined in the TV classic game show, Hollywood Squares.

In one scene, Marlon plays the ukulele adeptly, and sings with Wally the Irving Berlin song, Mr. Jazz Himself, and later, St. James Infirmary.
In addition to directing, [Rhoden] handled the sound effects like a pro.

Review from UpCurtain.com, Feb. 4, 2008.

Though not obscure, Wally Cox is certainly less well remembered than his childhood friend and perennial buddy, Marlon Brando. In Fletcher Rhoden's new play, set in Brando's study in 1974, Cox returns from the grave to visit his aging friend who, with a gun on his desk, may be contemplating suicide.

The two recall professional ups and downs, neglected children and abusive parents. Rhoden makes the case that childhood traumas are responsible for everything else. The first act climaxes with Brando asking Cox if he committed suicide.

The dialogue is leavened with duets, fake football games and the kind of horseplay they indulged in as kids. They deny tabloid rumors of homosexuality.

Frank Cavestani has the difficult task of representing the well-known Brando. Though he has the look, the bloated handsomeness and the mannerisms, he's still growing into the part. We're looking for the gravitas and mischievousness that Brando retained even into his final interview on the Larry King show.

The play is brightened by the deliciously funny Raf Mauro as Cox, who, with exquisite comic timing, makes us understand why Brando hated to see him go.

Performed on a nearly bare stage, this ghost play's eeriest moment comes at the end when Brando is alone, a knock comes at the door and a voice says, "Dad, it's Christian." The actor's son Christian Brando died last week and it's too bad he couldn't get to see his father's pain expressed here one last time.

from Joseph Mailander, Mayorsam.blogspot.com:

A funny and touching play is playing in the amiable church basement at Prospect and Rodney known as the Mt. Hollywood Theater: Last Tango with Marlon. Written by Fletcher Rhoden, who knew more than a few of those Hollywood Squares as a kid, and draws from some of that too. Raf Mauro as the ghost of Wally Cox is a constant delight. Notable aside at wikipedia: "Cox and Brando remained very close friends for the rest of Cox's life, and Brando is reported to have kept Cox's ashes in his bedroom and conversed with them nightly." Bet you didn't recall that Wally Cox and Marlon Brando were childhood friends, and maintained the friendship all the way up until Cox's death in the early 1970s. Brando's ashes were ultimately scattered with Cox's.

For THE TRIAL OF DAVY CROCKETT a fact-based novella (Trafford, 2001)

Review from The Midwest Book Review, November 11, 2001.
The Trial of Davy Crockett is a speculative fiction novella. Author Fletcher Rhoden questions whether Davy Crockett was truly killed during the battle for the Alamo -- or whether he was captured and executed by the Mexicans. The Trial of Davy Crockett presents a hypothetical dialogue between Crockett and Generalissimo Antonio López de Santa Anna, which collide in an articulate, wry, thought-provoking, and no-holds-barred verbal conflict regarding the Texian Revolution and America's unrestrained expansionism. Neither Crockett or Santa Anna is stereotyped in the roles of hero or villain; their opposing points of view are given a clear and fair hearing, for all to see and judge for themselves. Based entirely on the facts of the revolution, The Trial of Davy Crockett is a "must" for Texas history buffs and not to be missed.

Review from The Midwest Book Review's library newsletter, The Bookwatch, October 2001.
One of the obscure facts about the famous stand at the Alamo during the Texas war for liberation from Mexico is that Davy Crockett and a handful of others were captured alive by Santa Anna' forces when the mission-turned-fort fell. He and the others were summarily executed soon afterwards. Fletcher Rhoden has carefully crafted a novella that is based on the facts of the Texas revolution that gives fair and equal expression to both sides of

the conflict and is thoughtful yet riveting reading from first page to last.

The Trial of Davy Crockett: A Fascinating Meeting of Minds, January 27, 2002

By

Adrienne Armstrong (Fallbrook, CA USA)

I read "The Trial of Davy Crockett" by Fletcher Rhoden last week. From the moment I picked it up I couldn't put it down, and now that I've finished reading it I haven't been able to stop thinking about it. It's an extremely well-written and carefully-crafted piece, and the author obviously took great pains with his research. I'm interested in Texas history, but I'm certainly not an aficionado of the genre. What really fascinated me was the humanistic approach that Rhoden took with the meeting of these two larger-than-life historical characters, Davy Crockett and Generalissimo Antonio Lopez de Santa Anna, at the battle for the Alamo. It somehow combined the fanciful, what-if philosophy of "The Last Temptation of Christ" with the delicious possibilities presented in the best episodes of "Meeting of Minds or Steve Martin's wonderful play, "Picasso at the Lapin Agile". I recommend this book to anyone interested in American history, but more importantly, to anyone who enjoys a chance to listen in on what might have transpired between great men with great thoughts had they had the opportunity to really get into each other's heads.

Thought provoking view of Latino History, December 22, 2001

By "dgncc1701" (New York)

The Trial of Davy Crockett offers more than simply a must for Texas history buffs. In this novella, based in fact, author Fletcher Rhoden examines a dynamic character in Santa Anna and in so doing allows the reader a compelling account of Mexican history at a time when that country was shrinking under American expansionism. A subject all too often ignored by many American historians. The character of Davy Crockett does not wane in the shadow of Santa Anna. Written in a style so unique and intelligent, the reader cannot help but to keep turning the page. Santa Anna has become a sort of ogre in American eyes because of the slaughter at the Alamo and the brutality of the massacre at Goliad. The author's presentation of this dynamic historical period through the eyes of Santa Anna, definitely gives the reader a thought-provoking view of Latino History.

for THE CHRISTOPHER WALKEN ECSTATIC DANCE ACADEMY a dv short subject (Mighty One Prod. 2000)

L.A. Free For All by Gregory Weinkauf, Los Angeles New Times, March 8-14, 2001 "Best in show...*The Christopher Walken Ecstatic Dance Academy*... easily match[es] the best output of *Saturday Night Live* producer Lorne Michaels... A brief but intense encounter between a seemingly awkward fellow (Robbie Rist, an old friend of the director's whom many may remember as 'Cousin Oliver' from *The Brady Bunch*), his groovy girlfriend (Christy McBrayer), and the acting god, the movie features Quinton Flynn in the title role, sporting tics and mannerisms as thick as his prosthetic makeup. It's hilarious... and we're treated to [Rhoden's] immensely hummable tune, *Can't Stop Talkin' Like Christopher Walken*."

Blujesto Press Knows

Vol. 1

by

Fletcher Rhoden

Blujesto Press Knows Vol. 1
Fletcher Rhoden
c2014 Blujesto Press
fletcherrhoden@yahoo.com
blujestopress@yahoo.com

Also available from Fletcher Rhoden / Blujesto Press

HARD CELL: How to Use Proteins, Enzymes, Vitamins, Nutrients, Minerals, & Herbs for Superior Health

THE ART OF WAR, THE FIGHT FOR LOVE: How to Win the Love You Want and Keep the Love You Have

THE ART OF WAR, THE COLOR OF MONEY: How to Earn the Fortune You Want and Keep the Fortune You Have

FIFTY SHADES OF TRAILER PARK BOYS: TPB in the Great Comedic Traditions

A PROGRESSIVE CHRISTIAN HANDBOOK: How To Reconcile Your Scientific and Spiritual Beliefs (Jenni Frendswith)

SCHOOL XING

FREEDOM HALL

WARRIOR TIDE: Miguel de Cervantes at the Battle of Lepanto

NEVER DIE TWICE

THE NOVELLAS: The Trial Of Davy Crockett, Last Tango With Marlon

on DVD: WRITE MAKES MIGHT: Stronger Structure in Storytelling

Blujesto Press Knows Vol. 1:

EBOLA KNOWS: How to Survive 21
BANKSY KNOWS: Street Art 53
YELLOWSTONE KNOWS: Impending Doom 79
NIKOLA TESLA KNOWS: How to Invent the Future 103
EXCERPTS FROM OTHER BLUJESTO PRESS BOOKS 127

EBOLA KNOWS: How to Survive
Table of Contents

INTRODUCTION

PLAGUES FROM THE PAST What constitutes a plague? What we can learn from previous plagues, how they were handled, How the death rates compare to other plagues (so far)

EBOLA'S PAST Liberia, , Ebola timeline

EBOLA'S PRESENT Definition, symptoms, transmission, treatment, containment, sterilization, inconsistencies, Ebola's viral load, mutation, expiration

EBOLA'S FUTURE Travel restrictions and containment, screening, vaccines

WHAT CAN YOU DO?

EXCERPTS Samples of other Blujesto Press books

INTRODUCTION

Like a lot of biological success stories, including the Human race, the virus commonly called Ebola knows a lot. It knows how to survive, it knows how to evolve and meet rising challenges. It's a lot like us (though not actually a living species). And there's a lot we can learn from it. In fact, only when we understand it more thoroughly can we create the vaccines and protocols which can most effectively combat, control and constrain it.

And we'd better learn those things fast, because the very future of our life on this planet may depend on it.

The Ebola virus knows how to survive. And that's just what we all need to know when dealing with this powerful, mysterious, mercurial adversary. So though we know little of Ebola, we know much of where it comes from, where it thrives, and therefor where it may go. Knowing that, we may intercept and destroy it. Failing to know it, we may be outflanked and outwitted by a potentially devastating virus.

The human is a very successful species on its own, and it's survived many microbial threats before Ebola. But this virus isn't to be taken lightly, and knowing the virus better is to know how to control it. To put it another way, if you don't know what Ebola knows, you don't now how to survive.

So learn from the enemy how to defeat it by mastering the secrets of its own success. Know what it knows. And what Ebola knows is how to survive.

Now, so will you.

This brief but impactful volume will give you a thorough practical knowledge of how this modern-day plague works, what historical events made it possible, and what can be done to create a future free from its terrible threats.

PLAGUES FROM THE PAST What constitutes a plague, what we can learn from similar plagues and how they were handled, and how their death rates compare to Ebola (so far)

WHAT CONSTITUTES A PLAGUE

Even before we educate ourselves about the historical plagues and then on to a full understanding of the Ebola virus and the current outbreak, we should get some basic terminology straight.

PLAGUE: A highly infectious, usually fatal disease.

VIRUS: Any one of numerous submicroscopic agents that infect living organisms, usually causing disease. A virus consists of a single or double strand of RNA or DNA which are surrounded by a coat of protein. Because they are unable to replicate on their own (in other words,without a living host cell) viruses are not typically considered to be living organisms.

EPIDEMIC: Outbreak of disease which spreads very quickly and affects vast numbers of individuals, generally at the same time.

PANDEMIC: An epidemic occurring over a wide geographic area and usually affecting a very large proportion of the population.

So think of a pandemic is an epidemic on a geographical scale. But both share characteristics that distinguish them from other types of outbreaks:

- Quick Start
- Rapid Spread
- All Ages Affected
- Large Numbers Stricken
- High Death and Attack Rate

Plague of Justinian (541-542)

The bubonic plague outbreak spread quickly through the Byzantine Empire and centered on the Mediterranean region. It halted the reconquest of lands once part of the Roman Empire.

Cholera (1800s - present)

The Cholera pandemics began in India during the 1800s. The seventh (and still ongoing) outbreak began in Indonesia in 1961. It spread across Asia, to the Middle East, and on to Africa. This long-running disease may soon have a vaccine, however, according to the latest reports.

Typhus epidemic of 1847 (1847)

Ireland lost massive amounts of its citizenry during the epidemic. Others fled disease and the ensuing famine of 1846, but many died in so-called coffin ships. Many more perished on arrival as immigrants to various Canadian and U.S. ports.

Great Plague of London (1665-1666)

Twenty percent of Londoners died in this, the last of the London bubonic plagues going back to 1499. Early 1666 marked its recession and finally the Great Fire of London later that year virtually wiped the plague out, having incinerated many of the infected rodents and blankets.

Moscow Plague and Riot (1771)

The plague that started in late 1770 would turn into a major epidemic in 1771. The measures undertaken by the authorities caused anger and fear in the citizenry; destruction of contaminated property without control or compensation, forced quarantines, public baths closings, and more. Closing the city's many markets, factories, stores and other businesses and services paralyzed the economy. Food shortages followed, which helped erode living conditions among Muscovites. After an exodus, approximately 1000 people gathered at the Spasskiye gates on September 17, 1771. They demanded the elimination of quarantines and the release of captured rebels. The crowd was dispersed bodily by the army and several hundred people were put on trail. Order was restored in Moscow, and food and work pacified the Russian people.

Great Plague of Marseille (1720 – 1722)

Arriving in Marseille, France in 1720, the disease took 100,000 lives. But Marseille recovered fairly quickly. Economic activity returned after only a few short years. Trade expanded all the way to the West Indies and also to Latin America. The growing population was back at its pre-1720 level by 1765. A plague wall, the Mur de la Peste, was erected to subdivide the countryside.

Antonine Plague (165 – 180 CE)

The Antonine Plague (AKA the Plague of Galen, known to be the man who first and best described it), was an ancient and terrible pandemic. It's believed to have been a strain of either measles or smallpox, and was probably transmitted to Rome by troops on the march from the Near East. Two Roman emperors, Lucius Verus (died 169 CE) and Marcus Aurelius Antoninus, his co-regent (died 180 CE), perished from the dreaded disease. Antoninus' family name was given to the epidemic. (The name was also used for the character played by Tony Curtis in the 1960 film Spartacus.) Nine years later, the epidemic returned, causing as many as 2,000 deaths per day at Rome. The number equates to 25% of those infected. The death toll is estimated at roughly five million people. As many as 33% of the population died in many areas of the empire. It did severe damage to the Roman army.

Plague of Athens (430–427 BC)

The Plague of Athens hit Athens during the second year of the Peloponnesian War (430 BCE). Athenian victory still seemed possible, even probable. The plague is thought to have entered Athens through the city's port of Piraeus. The port was the only source of supplies and food. Sparta was also struck, as was much of the eastern Mediterranean. The plague returned in 429 BC and in 427 - 4366 BCE. The loss of this war likely made possible the later success of the Macedonians and, subsequently, the Romans. Long considered an outbreak of the bubonic plague, new candidates include smallpox, smallpox, toxic shock syndrome, and measles. Great Plague of Milan (1629–1631)

This series of bubonic plague outbreaks occurred in northern Italy from 1629 through 1631 and claimed roughly 280,000 lives, Venice and Lombardy endured notably high death rates during this, one of the last outbreaks of the centuries-long pandemic of bubonic plague which began with the Black Death. In 1629, German and French troops are known to have carried the plague to Mantua after the close of the Thirty Years' War (1618–1648). Infected with the disease, Venetian troops retreated into northern and central Italy. Milan suffered roughly 60,000 fatalities, almost half of their total population of only 130,000 people.

American Plagues (16th century)

Pandemics of measles and smallpox and other European diseases came along with the first large-scale contacts between Europeans and native American people. Sometimes these diseases even flourished ahead of actual contact with Europeans. The result was a plummeting population. In the 16th century, smallpox and other diseases wiped out the Aztec and Inca civilizations in South and Central America. The downfall of both American empires followed, in addition to the American peoples' subjugation to the white Europeans. Of course disease was a two-way street (then as now) and syphilis was carried back to Europe and nearly wiped out the population.

Great Plague of London (1665 – 1666)

75,000 to 100,000 people (20% of London's population) died in this plague, attributed to fleas carried on the backs of Norway rats. The Bubonic Plague was among the last widespread outbreaks of the disease to be found in England. Contemporary scholars suggest that the reported symptoms and recorded incubation period now indicate that the disease may have been similar to a viral hemorrhagic fever, or Ebola virus.

Plague of Justinian (541 – 542)

In 541 and 542 CE, the Plague of Justinian afflicted the Byzantine Empire as the Christians never could, including its capital Constantinople. Most people believed bubonic plague was the cause, and that it later caused or contributed to the 14th century's Black Death. The Plague of Justinian was very nearly worldwide in its scope (the known world anyway), hitting south and central Asia, Arabia, North Africa, and Europe. Even Denmark and Ireland were hit. Until 750, the plague returned consistently throughout the Mediterranean basin. At the zenith of the pandemic, the plague killed upwards of 5,000 people per day in Constantinople. As many as 40% of the city's inhabitants and a quarter of the human population of the eastern Mediterranean eventually died.

The Third Pandemic (1855 – 1950s)

Beginning in 1855 China, this episode of bubonic plague ultimately killed more than 12 million people in China and India alone. Considered active until as recently as 1959, worldwide casualties dropped to 200 per year. The plague was endemic in central Asian populations of infected ground rodents. It was a known cause of death among established and migrant human populations. Most experts agree that the Black Death is lying dormant and will make a strong return to the global landscape soon.

The Black Death (1347 – 1351)

Also known as The Black Plague or Bubonic Plague, the Black Death remains one of the deadliest pandemics in history. Many believe that the pandemic began in Central Asia or China in the late 1320s or 1330s. Later, soldiers and merchants carried it over caravan routes. By1346 it had reached the Crimea. However, the plague may have been endemic to southern Russia. Regardless, the plague spread to North Africa and to Western Europe during the 1340s. As many as 75 million people may have died worldwide, roughly 25–50 million in Europe. And this plague wasn't alone; more than 100 plague epidemics are known to have swept across Europe at this time.

The 1918 Influenza Pandemic (1918-1919)

The virus which came to be known as Spanish Flu killed scores of people (estimated at somewhere between 20 and 50 million) all over the world. It is one of the worst epidemics in human history.

HIV/AIDS (1959 - present)

HIV (Human Immunodeficiency Virus) and AIDS (Acquired Immune Deficiency Syndrome) are part of a cycle (AIDS develops from HIV) of infection. HIV is transmitted by exposure to an infected person's bodily fluids. This can occur via intimate contact such as intercourse. It may also be transmitted by blood transfusion with infected blood, or by intravenous drug use. It takes roughly nine years for HIV to lead to a case of so-called full-blown AIDS. HIV may be spread through vertical transmission (from mother to her newborn baby) at birth and even through breast milk. First positively identified in 1959 in the Congo, the disease remains incurable. However, some success in slowing the progress of the development from HIV to AIDS has been seen in many recent cases.

HOW THEY WERE HANDLED

Vaccines are the ideal way to end an epidemic. Smallpox, polio, whooping cough and others indicate that vaccines can be effective and fast-working, although there is some controversy over the side effects of certain vaccines, believed to cause autism and other conditions.

The Spanish flu epidemic was managed by shuttering public places and schools and imposing quarantines. Libraries stopped lending books, even handshaking was warmed against, though not prohibited. Like a lot of the epidemics, the cycle simply ran its course once those who suffered from it died or recovered and others developed or already had immunity.

What helped curtail the spread of HIV/AIDS was a combination of education, behavioral modification and advances in pharmaceutical "cocktails," different combinations of drugs. But the disease remains widespread and dangerous, and continued diligence and experimentation will be required before a vaccine can be found.

The end of the Black Death is attributed to many things: Improved medical practices, better hygiene, winter weather (which discourages the fleas which carried the disease to humans), also the Great London Fire probably did a lot to wipe out the infected rats who carried those fleas (rats are known to be the reservoir of the bubonic plague at that time). The fire also destroyed infected blankets. It's important to remember that bubonic plague still exists today, and can be found in rodents in California and other highly developed areas.

Like bubonic plague, most of these other plague viruses simply receded, then returned later with even more lethality. So when or while the current outbreak of Ebola may indeed be contained, the probability of its return is always looming.

HOW THE DEATH RATES OF OTHER PLAGUES COMPARE TO EBOLA (SO FAR)

It's vital to understand the toll Ebola exacts in relation to the other plagues. Here are the numbers of fatalities for some of these plagues or outbreaks:

Plague of Justinian (541-542) 100,000,000
Black Plague (1346 - 1350) 50,000,000
HIV/AIDS (1959-present) 39,000,000
Flu of 1918 (1918-1929) 50,000,000
Modern Plague (1894 - 1903) 10,000,000
Ebola: (1976 - present) 4,500

The numbers make Ebola seem quite harmless, but remember that almost all of these Ebola deaths have occurred in the recent outbreaks, over a relatively brief period. The possibilities for the future of these statistics are staggering and have to be considered.

EBOLA'S PAST Liberia, a comparison to other plagues (so far), Ebola timeline

LIBERIA

Think of Liberia as Ground Zero for Ebola. This is where Thomas Eric Duncan, the first patient diagnosed with Ebola in the U.S., contracted the virus before coming to Texas. In Liberia, the Ebola virus has 4,665 recorded cases and 2,705 deaths.

So it's important to understand a little bit about Liberia (where the virus is so successful) so that we can predict how successful the virus will be elsewhere, such as the United States, Canada, Europe and other more highly developed parts of the world.

Featuring rain forests, soft sand beaches and mountain peaks, Liberia is about the same size as Kentucky. Liberia, on the West African coast, borders Sierra Leone, Guinea, and Côte d'Ivoire. The World Bank has estimated Liberia's population to be roughly 4.3 million people, with over 3 million of them living in Monrovia, the capital.

In 1822, 86 emigrants traveled with the American Colonization Society to the coast of West Africa. The WCS had been founded six years earlier, with the goal of sending American-born black citizens back to Africa. The settlement was renamed Monrovia, after then president and ACS member James Monroe.

Liberia declared its independence from the ACS in 1847. Virginia-born black American Joseph J. Roberts became Liberia's first president. Liberia was the only free republic in Africa at this time.

In the 1990s Charles Taylor (who is now serving a half-century sentence in a Rwandan prison for war crimes) and his rebel group National Patriotic Front of Liberia (NPFL) assassinated Doe and seized control of most of the country. A 1995 peace agreement installed Taylor as president. According to the UN, Liberia traded diamonds for weapons with rebels in Sierra Leone. In 2003 Taylor was exiled to Nigeria.

Liberia President Ellen Johnson Sirleaf came to power in 2006, and she won re-election in 2011. Sirleaf fought corruption by Liberia's leadership and brought foreign investments into the country. Liberia remains quite poor (1.3 million citizens live in extreme poverty), and the Ebola crisis has highlighted just how desperately it needs both hospital beds and qualified doctors. The CIA's World Factbook estimates that there is one doctor for every 100,000 people in Liberia, compared to 242 doctors for every 100,000 people in the United States.

But a crumbling infrastructure contributes as much to the Ebola outbreak as does the anemic medical care available. Poor roads have hindered transport of patients and medical equipment. Summers in Liberia are very stormy, which mean that floods block these meager roads. Closed borders make vital supplies even harder to get.

There is also the matter of drought. Ebola is a disease which causes massive fluid loss, resulting in organ failure and death. And Liberia, like many African nations (and nations all over the world) has limited supplies of clean drinking water. Dehydration is a danger when suffering from the Ebola virus, and experts agree that staying hydrated to maintain the body's integrity through the difficult illness can vastly increase the chances of survival. Not staying hydrated can likewise contribute to the deadly toll of the disease and thwart the body's efforts to fight the virus. Death is the likely result of this course, as Liberia demonstrates.

And along with drought, malnutrition contributes to the diseases's destructive tendencies in the same way. The body loses proteins, enzymes and vitamins it needs to fight the disease, and unless these are replenished the body is unlikely to survive the battle. Famine-stricken and drought-plagued, with poor waste management and a crumbling infrastructure, Liberia was the perfect breeding ground for this treacherous virus.

EBOLA OUTBREAK 2014 TIMELINE

To bring the past up to date and deliver us seamlessly into the present, let's take a look at the timeline of Ebola's rise and spread. That will bring us into a discussion of the virus's current state and its possible future.

- March 22: Previously unidentified hemorrhagic fever, confirmed in Guinea, which killed more than 50 people, was identified as Ebola.

- March 30: Two Ebola cases were reported in Liberia; Sierra Leone reports numerous suspected cases.

- April 1: Medecins Sans Frontieres (MSF), a medical charity, warned the epidemic's spread was unprecedented. A World Health Organization (WHO) spokesman called it, "Relatively small."

- April 4: Guinea Ebola treatment center was attacked by a mob, driven by fear and superstition about the disease, with other hostilities against healthcare workers in Sierra Leone and Liberia.

- May 26: First Ebola deaths in Sierra Leone were confirmed by WHO.

- June 17: Ebola was reported in the Liberian capital of Monrovia.

- June 23: MSF reported over 350 deaths, making the West African outbreak the worst on record.

- July 25: First Ebola case was confirmed in Nigeria, a man who had travelled shortly before from Monrovia.

- July 29: Dr. Sheik Umar Khan died of Ebola. Dr. Khan had been leading Sierra Leone's fight against the epidemic.

- July 30: Troops enforced school closings and quarantines in the effected areas of Liberia.

- August 2: A U.S. missionary physician infected with Ebola in Liberia, Kent Brantly, was flown to Atlanta in the United States for treatment.

- August 5: A second U.S. missionary reported to be infected with Ebola, Nancy Writebol, was flown from Liberia to Atlanta for treatment.

- August 8: Ebola was declared an international public health emergency by WHO.

- Aug. 12: Death toll tops 1,000, WHO approves use of unproven drugs or vaccines. A Spanish priest with Ebola died in Madrid hospital.

- August 15: MSF reported that the Ebola epidemic in West Africa will take about six months to control.

- August 20: Security forces in Monrovia disperse a crowd trying to break out of quarantine, killing a teenager with use of tear gas and gunfire.

- August 21: Two U.S. missionary aid workers treated in Atlanta, Brantly and Writebol, were released from hospital August 19 and 21 declared to be entirely free of the Ebola virus.

- August 24: The Ebola outbreak was declared in the Democratic Republic of Congo. This outbreak was believed to be separate from West Africa epidemic. On the same day, an infected British medical worker was flown home from Sierra Leone for treatment.

- August 28: Death toll climbed above 1,550 death toll, according to WHO, which warned that outbreak could still infect more than 20,000 people overall.

- August 29: The first confirmed Ebola case was reported in Senegal.

- September 2: MSF president condemned global inaction and also warned the United Nations that the world was losing the battle to contain the spread of Ebola.

- September 3: Deaths topped 1,900, with officials estimating 400 deaths in that week alone. On that day, the third U.S. missionary doctor infected with the Ebola virus was flown from Liberia to Omaha, Nebraska for treatment.

- September 5: Death toll topped 2,100 out of roughly 4,000 people thought to have been infected, according to WHO.

- September 7: President Barack Obama publicly agreed that the United States needed to do more to prevent the Ebola epidemic from becoming a full-blown global crisis.

- September 8: Britain decided to set up a treatment center in Sierra Leone and to dispatch military and humanitarian experts; United States agreed to contribute the services of a field hospital to care for healthcare workers in Liberia. On that day, the fourth Ebola patient was flown to United States for treatment in Atlanta.

- September 9: Death toll passed 2,296 out of 4,293 cases recorded in five countries.

- September 12: Cuba announced it would train and send 165 doctors and nurses to Sierra Leone to treat Ebola patients.

- September 13: Liberia appealed to President Obama for aid to fight Ebola.

- September 16: United States committed 3,000 military engineers and medical personnel to West Africa to build clinics and train healthcare workers.

- WHO reported 2,461 people dead out of 4,985 infected, doubling the Ebola death toll in the past month.

- September 17: MSF reported that French nurse volunteer in Liberia had Ebola. Her name had not been released as of the November 1 2014 publication of this book.

- September 18: Death toll rose to 2,630 dead out of 5,357 believed infected, according to WHO. Security Council adopted resolution calling for lifting travel, border restrictions while the United Nations sent special mission staffs to combat Ebola in Liberia, Guinea, and Sierra Leone. French President Francois Hollande committed to setting up a military hospital in Guinea.

- September 19: Sierra Leone's capital, Freetown, was put under three-day lockdown in an attempt to halt the spread of the Ebola virus.

- September 20: Liberian Thomas Eric Duncan flew from Liberia (to Dallas via Brussels and Washington) after he tried to help a woman infected with Ebola in his home country.

- September 22: Senegal and Nigeria outbreaks were declared contained by WHO, reports Ebola deaths at more than 2,811 people in West Africa.

- September 23: U.S. Centers for Disease Control and Prevention (CDC) estimated between 550,000 and 1.4 million people in West Africa may have Ebola by January, 2015.

- September 25: Duncan went to Dallas hospital with abdominal pain and fever. Despite telling a nurse he'd just arrived from West Africa, he was sent home.

- September 26: Death toll was elevated to 3,091 dead out of 6,574 probable, suspected and confirmed cases, according to WHO. Cuba committed to training 296 more doctors and nurses to treat Ebola patients in West Africa. 165 were already preparing to go to Sierra Leone at that time.

- September 28: Duncan was returned by ambulance to Dallas hospital.

- September 30: CDC confirmed that Duncan had Ebola; the first case of the disease to be diagnosed in the United States.

- October 1: Official death toll rises to 3,338 dead out of 7,178 cases in West Africa, according to WHO. Cuba made good on its commitment and sent 165 Ebola trained doctors and nurses to Sierra Leone.

- October 2: Britain pleaded for international help to fight epidemic at conference in London. NBC News said American freelance cameraman in its employ, Ashoka Mukpo, was reported to have the Ebola virus. Mukpo would be flown to the United States for treatment.

- October 3: Death toll rose to 3,439 dead out of 7,492 suspected, probable and confirmed cases in West Africa and one case in the United States, according to WHO. That day, the Ugandan doctor with Ebola arrived in Frankfurt from Sierra Leone for treatment.

- October 4: The first French national to contract Ebola, a volunteer nurse, left a hospital outside Paris after being successfully treated for the disease.

- October 6: A Spanish nurse, Teresa Romero, was reported to be infected with Ebola; she had previously treated an infected Spanish priest who was repatriated to Madrid and died. On that day, cameraman Mukpo in Omaha was taken to Nebraska Medical Center.

- October 8: Duncan, the first person diagnosed with Ebola in the United States, died in a Dallas hospital. That same day, the U.S. government ordered five major airports to screen passengers from West Africa for fever.

- October 9: Death toll was elevated to 3,865 out of 8,033 cases, according to WHO, which reported there was no evidence that the epidemic was being brought under control in West Africa, contrary to previous reports. Britain declared it would screen passengers entering country through London's two main airports and also through the Eurostar rail link with the European nations. Egged on by the news, lawmakers called for the United States to ban travelers from the West African countries hit hardest by Ebola.

- October 10: The death toll climbed up to 4,033 out of 8,399 cases in seven countries, according to WHO.

- October 11: New York's John F. Kennedy International airport began screening travelers from three West African countries for Ebola symptoms.

- October 12: Nurse Nina Pham in Dallas tested positive for Ebola, becoming first person to contract the virus in the United States. She was infected while caring for Duncan at Texas Health Presbyterian Hospital.

- October 14: Britain began screening travelers from West Africa at Heathrow, London's busiest airport. On that day, Sudanese U.N. medical official and Ebola patient died in German hospital. He'd contracted the disease in Liberia.

- October 15: Amber Vinson was the second Texas nurse who treated Duncan to be reported as having contracted Ebola. Vinson was treated at

Emory University Hospital in Atlanta. Authorities said Vinson took flight from Cleveland to Dallas/Fort Worth International Airport while running slight fever. Death toll rose to 4,493 people out of 8,997 cases, according to WHO, which reported that the Ebola epidemic was at that time still spreading in West Africa.

- October 16: A U.S. congressional subcommittee questioned health officials about response to Ebola in United States. Nurse Pham would be moved from Dallas to an isolation unit in Bethesda, Maryland.

- October 17: Death toll was elevated to 4,546 people out of 9,191 cases of Ebola, according to WHO. That day, Senegal was reported not to have the Ebola virus while U.S. President Barack Obama appointed the first Ebola czar, Ron Klain.

- October19: Spanish nurse appeared to be entirely free of the Ebola virus.

- October 20: Nigeria was officially (if temporarily) declared to be free and clear of the Ebola virus. That day in Texas, as many as 43 individuals were taken off watch lists. Meanwhile, United States issued more strident and comprehensive guidelines for healthcare workers who were or are treating Ebola victims, to mandate that no skin or hair be exposed.

- October 21: Medicins Sans Frontieres reported it would start trials of experimental Ebola drugs at its new West African treatment centers the following month. Cuba sent 53 doctors and nurses to Liberia and another 38 to Guinea to treat Ebola patients. Meanwhile, the U.S. announced that starting Oct. 22 all travelers to the United States from Liberia, Sierra Leone and Guinea must fly into one of five designated airports for enhanced screening. Ashoka Mukpo, the NBC freelance cameraman, was declared to be free of the virus and was scheduled to leave the hospital shortly thereafter.

- October 22: United States announced that anyone entering the country from the three nations at the center of the epidemic would have to endure 21 days of controlled subject monitoring.

- October 23: New York City doctor, Dr. Craig Spencer, who treated patients in Guinea, was tested positive for the deadly Ebola virus. First cases of Ebola were reported in Mali, the sixth West African nation hit by the virus.

- October 24: Dallas nurse Nina Pham was declared to be free of the Ebola virus and left the hospital. Spencer was at New York's Bellevue Hospital, remaining in isolation. Bellevue was one of eight hospitals statewide designated by New York Gov. Andrew Cuomo as part of an Ebola preparedness plan.

- October 27: The U.S. Army started isolating soldiers who were returning from an Ebola response mission in West Africa. At least six states issued tougher rules for travelers returning from Ebola-affected regions, some with mandatory quarantines going above and beyond federal guidelines.

- October 29: California adopted guidelines for containment / quarantine based on New York / New Jersey and other state protocols.

And that brings us right up until the present, the events that have led us to what may well be the precipice, the edge of the cliff. Or, frankly, it may not be. To better understand how Ebola currently effects our lives, and how it will continue to effect our lives, we must now turn our attention to the virus itself. What is it, how does it spread, and how can it be contained?

EBOLA'S PRESENT Definition, symptoms, transmission, treatment, containment, sterilization, inconsistencies, Ebola's viral load, mutation, expiration

DEFINITION

Ebola hemorrhagic fever, usually called Ebola or Ebola virus, is an often-fatal disease caused by a virus. African bats are believed to have originated (and may still be a reservoir for) the virus.

Symptoms (in chronological order) include:

- Fever
- Muscle Pain and weakness
- Bleeding
- Severe sore throat
- Jaundice
- Stomach pain
- Vomiting
- Severer Diarrhea
- Organ failure
- Death

TRANSMISSION

According to experts and the latest information, people infected with Ebola are contagious only when they are showing symptoms. The virus is spread through contact with infected:

- Blood
- Urine
- Saliva
- Semen
- Sweat

The fluids must have an entry point into the body, such as the eyes, nose, ears, mouth, an open cut on the skin.

Ebola is not believed to be transmittable in the air, such as by a sneeze or a cough (unless there is direct open-entry contact as described above). Therefore Ebola is not likely to be transmitted in a public place, such as a subway car, office building or passenger plane, according to experts and current date.

TREATMENT

There is no specific treatment for Ebola. The idea instead is to treat symptoms so as to give the body more time to fight the infection. Since fluid loss is prevalent in Ebola sufferers, fluids, nutrients and medicines are administered. Experimental treatments have been tried on several patients, but no discernible effect has been noted yet.

CONTAINMENT

Containment of Ebola is possible, but it's not going to be easy by anyone's estimation. But a lot of experts do agree with the isolation of possibly infected individuals. Those with whom a potentially infected person has had contact should check their body temperature twice a day for three weeks, which is the incubation period for the disease. Isolation and testing is recommended for those who do show symptoms during that three-week period.

STERILIZATION

The good news is that Ebola is not an especially hearty virus outside of the body. It can be killed on most surfaces with hospital-grade disinfectants and common household bleach.

INCONSISTENCIES

This new strain of Ebola may (or may not) be more contagious or heartier than other strains. The fact is, the virus has only been known since 1976, and several varying strains do exist (some reports account for as many as 300).

But this particular strain simply hasn't been studied that thoroughly, and neither has the disease in general. So, unlike influenza or HIV/AIDS, we just haven't had the time to learn more about this aggressive and adaptive virus.

The virus is inconsistent. Some infected with Ebola never even take ill. Some who do become sick go on to shed massive amounts of virus and are particularly contagious. They're known in the world of viruses as super-shedders. While most people are not super-shedders, they can spread the disease as well, but with less effectiveness. Fever is widely reported to be the first symptom of Ebola virus disease (during which time the patient can be considered contagious). However, sometimes the fever lags behind other symptoms, or never even appears over the course of the illness.

Ebola mutates, the same way all viruses do. But since we know so little about this virus, and since it has been so successful in so short a time, there's no way to know whether the virus will mutate, how it may do so, or how fast it may do so. Experts agree that there is a remote possibility that significant mutation would greatly enhance the virus's spread over the entire globe. This possibility does seem remote, but the stakes are astronomical.

Because of the virus's unpredictability, experts agree that instances of asymptomatic infection may occur; a person may become infected with Ebola and never develop symptoms, thus they never become contagious. In these cases, the patient is likely to recover fully and be virus-free ... without ever knowing they'd had the virus in the first place.

EBOLA'S VIRAL LOAD

There's also the question of Ebola's viral load. Virus particles are capable of being infectious, which means they can take hold in another living system. But that's not the same thing as being contagious, which means they can travel successfully from one living system to another. As we have discussed, Ebola is transmitted through direct contact with bodily fluids. It is not known to be an airborne contagion, like measles or influenza.

But some experts now believe that Ebola has a significantly higher viral load than most other contagions. With more virus present in every drop of fluid, this virus will be more contagious than other viruses which are transmitted in the same manner. It would also indicate that the virus can replicate faster than comparable viruses, making it prone to more varied and stronger, more resilient mutations.

And there's another troubling factor to the question of Ebola's viral load. New evidence indicates that unlike a lot of comparable viruses, Ebola's viral load increases as the disease progresses. This explains why an infected individual without symptoms will not spread the virus initially: There's not that much virus present in the blood, and it is not yet present in other bodily fluids. It may be many days before it makes its way to the bladder and begins to be detectable in urine.

The question of when an infected person begins to shed the virus, and especially in what quantity, is an extremely important one for obvious reasons. Since symptoms begin much sooner than urinal or fecal residue is likely to spread it, the virus's most dangerous times are when the patient is still likely to be in the general population, a time during which the patient is contagious.

MUTATION

What would be even more alarming, scientists say, is if Ebola somehow mutated to become an airborne virus. As we've seen, many experts agree that it is very unlikely that Ebola will change its mode of transmission. But if it did, experts also agree that the entire world population could be in terrible danger.

Viruses rarely mutate in their form of transmission, which is what this virus would have to do to become airborne. What's more, the Ebola virus in particular does not have an affinity for the cells deep in the lungs. That makes it a poor candidate for respiratory transmission.

But Ebola's current success does indicate the stronger possibility of mutation, by sheer force of numbers. All viruses evolve and mutate through generations, like any other living thing. With so many deaths happening so quickly (this outbreak alone has claimed a reported 4,500 lives, though that report varies), the virus has more opportunities to evolve and mutate. And given those opportunities, a lack of evolution or mutation actually seems unlikely.

But if Ebola does mutate (and that does seem likely), experts are inclined to agree that the evolution will not be in its mode of transmission, rather in the lifecycle of the virus and its host. Most virologists agree that the key to a stronger success of the virus is to have the host die more slowly, so that it can have a longer, more active contagious period. At present, the hosts die fairly quickly (when they do die) and that limits the virus's ability to transmit from person to person.

So the current epidemic is likely due to human responses to the disease (containment policies, for example) rather than to the responses of the virus itself (evolution and mutation). So it's not that the Ebola virus is mutating too fast, we're just having a hard time dealing with it. So far.

But make no mistake, the Ebola is mutating. And the increasing secondary infection rate (household members who may contract the virus from an infected individual) will indicate just how much it's mutating, and now fast.

EXPIRATION

Three further strains have been identified: Reston virus, Taï Forest virus (formerly known as Côte d'Ivoire Ebolavirus) and Bundibugyo virus. The Zaire and Sudan strains are the two most-common cause of human infections, with Zaire boasting up to 90% fatalities. Curiously, Reston is the only Ebola virus not currently known to be pathogenic in humans.

Ebola is closely related to Marburg, identified in 1967. Marburg is extremely virulent, like Ebola, causing a hemorrhagic fever that frequently proves deadly.

Ebola first infects the leucocytes, or white blood cells. Then it attacks nearly any and every other type of cell. This is what makes the virus so spectacularly deadly; no cell may be immune. This process typically takes between two and 21 days, with death occurring six to 16 days after the onset of the illness.

It's not a pretty sight. The first symptoms include fever, headache and fatigue. The virus overwhelms even more cells, and they simply burst, releasing chemicals which lead to terrible inflammation and, soon thereafter, toxic shock. The viral load increases, as mentioned before, and patients begin to suffer stomach pains. These are followed by bloody diarrhea, jaundice, severe sore throats, and vomiting. The immune system goes into overdrive. It launches a counter-attack which causes even more damage. Cells infected with this virus then attach themselves to the insides of veins, arteries, vessels, weakening them until they ultimately leak their vital fluids. This causes the dramatic fall in blood pressure and the multiple organ failure that's so well known and so feared. Uncontrollable hemorrhaging follows in over 50% of known cases. All these fluids can seep from the mouth and nose and eyes, creating the fabled tears of blood.

Victims go from being dazed to convulsing in agony, heaving bloody discharges from their stomachs called black vomit, recalling yellow fever or cholera.

EBOLA'S FUTURE Travel restrictions and containment, Screening, Vaccines

TRAVEL RESTRICTIONS AND CONTAINMENT

This is one of the most controversial aspects of the Ebola virus epidemic of 2014 ... and beyond. The problem with isolation has already been demonstrated. To restrict travel into Liberia and other West African hotbeds of the Ebola virus is to restrict access to the only resources that may help defeat the disease there. If the disease is allowed to spread unchecked, as it has, it will only flourish and continue to spread worldwide. It will also become stronger the longer it has to evolve and mutate far removed from outside antagonism.

The reasons for this are clear: Borders can never be locked off entirely. There will always be a violation of any containment policy, no matter how well executed or well intentioned. Infected individuals will still manage to get through, even if much-needed expertise and materials cannot. That's another thing Ebola knows that we don't seem to.

Even so:

Illinois joined New Jersey and New York and imposed mandatory quarantines for people arriving with a risk of having contracted Ebola in West Africa.

By October 27, The U.S. Army had started isolating soldiers who were returning from an Ebola response mission in West Africa. They didn't show any symptoms of infection and they were not believed to have been exposed to Ebola virus, by all official accounts.

The decision went well beyond previously established military protocols and they came just as President Obama's administration tried to discourage precautionary quarantines from being imposed by U.S. states. These quarantines were likely to prohibit healthcare workers from returning from Ebola-battling countries.

The Army presumed to isolate roughly a dozen soldiers upon their return to their Vicenza, Italy home base. The Army's isolation of its soldiers reflects a growing anxiety in the United States and abroad about Ebola's potential transmission worldwide. At this time, the Army is the only U.S. military service to order isolation, But armed forces are considering similar measures across the board.

According to a memo dated October 10, current Defense Department policy required troops with no known exposure to the virus to return to work and interact with their families after coming home, as long as they check their temperature twice daily for a period of 21 days.

By October 27, at least six states had issued tougher rules for travelers returning from Ebola-affected regions, some with mandatory quarantines going above and beyond federal guidelines.

The governors of New York and New Jersey announced mandatory quarantines for all travelers who had close contact with Ebola-infected individuals and were arriving from the three countries hardest hit by the virus: Guinea, Liberia and Sierra Leone.

A mandatory 21- day home quarantine for high-risk individuals who cared for Ebola patients in those same countries was announced by the Illinois Department of Public Health the same day.

Home quarantines with twice-daily monitoring from health officials would be allowed in New York and New Jersey. According to a statement made by New York Gov. Andrew Cuomo, mandatory hospital quarantines would only be required of high-risk individuals arriving to New York and New Jersey who were not from either of those states.

At this time (late October, 2014) Maine, Florida, Maryland, and Virginia also announced tougher rules for travelers returning from Ebola-affected regions. Home quarantine remained a strong possibility.

Nurse Kaci Hickox was returning from Sierra Leone, where she treated Ebola patients. She was detained and interrogated at New Jersey's Newark

Liberty International Airport. Although Hickox had no symptoms, she was held against her will and then ultimately released.

As of Oct. 22, 2014, the CDC would require airline passengers traveling from Ebola-affected nations to get Ebola kits. They would also be required to self-monitor for 21 days (the maximum incubation period). They were (and remain at the time of this publishing) required to take their temperature twice daily and they must also answer questions about their symptoms. Officials said they would be tracked down if they do not report voluntarily.

But quarantines bring up a lot of tangled legal and constitutional issues, of course.

The U.S. Constitution does empower the government to isolate ill individuals entering the country or in interstate travel, the states must truly regulate public health, and this includes enforcing quarantines within state borders.

In a first-ever move, the CDC recommended 21 days of isolation in addition to travel restrictions for those why may have a higher risk of having the Ebola virus even if they show absolutely no symptoms.

New Jersey issued an order similar to one in the neighboring state of New York, which requires a three-week quarantine for any person who treated any Ebola patients anywhere in West Africa. These people are not just those formerly deemed high-risk simply due of a needle-prick or a failure to use the proper protective safety gear. Under these new federal guidelines, many low-risk workers are only required to have their body temperatures taken twice daily.

New Jersey and New York could be facing significant legal challenges. To justify the infringement upon any individual's civil liberties, such as the freedom of movement, a state must prove that the order is based upon sound epidemiology and science. California adopted similar protocols toward the end of October, 2014.

Broad quarantines are rare in the United States and are generally limited to airborne diseases.

The so-called Spanish flu influenza virus infected millions of people in 1918. Schools were closed and strict quarantines were imposed in major U.S. cities across the nation. New York very nearly quarantined tuberculosis patients in the 1990s. Some who would not comply with treatment were in fact isolated.

SCREENING

The Otago Daily Times reported that a team of New Zealand researchers have developed a light-weight, mobile device called Freedom4, said to be able to accurately locate and identify traces of viruses and bacteria. This has only been possible through huge machines.

Medical equipment already existed to detect Ebola in New Zealand and elsewhere in the world, the necessary tests required burdensome equipment. This new device, however, is light and battery-powered, and it can send results back to the laboratory seamlessly via smartphone.

Since Ebola my travel so easily and therefor spread so quickly, devices like Freedom4 may prove essential in stopping it. Clearly, field testing is invaluable in the containment of viral outbreaks like Ebola.

Special emergency protocols and preparedness programs were emphasized in the United States after the attacks on September 11th and the ensuing anthrax scare. The research and the development of anti-viral drugs and vaccines were principle among those protocols.

Unfortunately, impediments included both budgetary constraints, partisan politics, and a fractured governmental system which left no one agency to spearhead the campaign against the epidemic. These combined to delay new protocols and preparedness systems from being put into place in the wake of the Ebola virus outbreak of 2014.

The back-to-back administrations of President Bill Clinton and President George W. Bush both had a White House senior position specifically to spearhead the effort to respond to natural pandemics and biological attacks, but the position was eliminated by the administration of Barack Obama.

However, in addition to a new Ebola czar (democrat Ron Klain) there are now roughly 24 presidentially appointed officials responsible for emergency response to the outbreaks of infectious and deadly disease.

Budget cuts also have slowed progress at the local level.

Since 2002, the U.S. CDC has reportedly given roughly $10 billion for public health systems to help prepare them for major disease outbreaks. But all states in the U.S., and numerous major cities, also received (and still receive) annual funding via the HHS's reputable Hospital Preparedness Program. This funding has helped numerous private hospitals to further develop various plans to handle the anticipated surging volume in emergency rooms and shelters across the country. The program has distributed a rough total of $5 billion to date. Annual funding, however, has fallen to roughly 50% since its 2003 peak. That year saw a distribution of roughly $515 million, indicating Congress's waning enthusiasm for the funding of bio-defense projects in general.

Meanwhile, significant budget cuts at the state level (not to mention a congressional sequester) also forced many U.S. states to eliminate various emergency protocols and preparedness systems. Funding limitations also contributed to a good deal of the long delay in vaccine development.

VACCINES

In the interests of circumventing the virus's difference in strains, scientists are trialling a possible vaccine using genetic material from both the Zaire and Sudan strains. The Canadians, meanwhile, are employing vesicular stomatitis virus (VSV), also an animal virus, to deliver genetic Ebola material for use in vaccine production.

The Canadians' experimental vaccine is known as VSV-EBOV.

Johnson & Johnson also announced it was investing $200 million in developing a two-step Ebola vaccine together with the Denmark-based biotechnology company Bavarian Nordic. That particular protocol requires taking two injections; the first is meant to prime the human immune system, while the second one boosts the first injection. Johnson & Johnson has announced plans to begin human trials in January 2015 and has promised it could have 250,000 doses available to the general public by May of that same year.

The WHO, meanwhile, has said that it hoped to make a serum vaccine using antibodies from the blood of Ebola survivors available in Liberia well before the end of 2014.

The question really is one of timing. Given enough time and enough raw viral material, vaccines will eventually be found. More vaccines will follow and the race against the virus's evolution may be won. However, experts agree that the question is whether the race will be lost before it has really begun. The danger is a scenario wherein a vaccine is shown to be safe and effective but can't be made widely available for several months or even a year thereafter. And by that time, there is always the chance that the next outbreak of Ebola will be caused by a completely different strain of the virus, against which current vaccines could be ineffective.

One silver lining to that grim scenario is that even if current vaccines are too late for this outbreak, finding them would put us substantially further along when the next outbreak occurs; not if, but when.

The Ebola virus's peculiarities, inconsistencies, and the sheer newness of the virus, all have important implications for vaccine design. Different strains of the virus may require different vaccines; by the time those vaccines are ready, the strains may already have mutated enough to be immune.

As you can see, Ebola really does know a lot. And one thing Ebola is an absolute genius at is evading the human immune system. Ebola uses two proteins, VP35 and VP24, to do this. The first protein enables the virus's long filament-like strands to form a spiral DNA-like shape that serves as a kind of viral invisibility cloak. VP24 then blocks the release of the protein interferon, which signals the presence of a foreign pathogen and kick-starts the immune response.

Half of Ebola's mass is actually carbohydrate, the compound which provides energy for human cells. In the same way Ebola hides from the body by using VP35 and VP24 proteins, it hides behind its own carbohydrate composition.

Once inside the cell, the virus hijacks enzymes in the cell. But by then the virus in embedded in the cell, and can replicate using the cell's own reproductive properties. This results in millions of copies of Ebola-embedded cells.

At this point, if the body's immune system can outrun the replication of infected cells, the virus may be defeated. If not, the process goes on in the manner described earlier in this book. What is important to remember here is that the virus is hard to detect because it knows how to hide; the same feature makes it very hard to find a vaccine for.

CONCLUSION

This is a good news/bad news situation. The bad news is that there's very little you can do. As an individual, your only chance to really help stem the tide of this virus's continued success is to go to West Africa and help stop the problem at its source. Other than that, the best you'll be able to do is survive.

And that's the good news; survival seems quite likely for you, and most of the human race, at least as far as this round of Ebola outbreaks is concerned. And there are things you can do, one of which you're already doing. Learning from previous epidemics, we know that we should stay educated (and reading this book is a great step in that direction) and make sure not to fall prey to any myths or common misunderstandings which cause unreasonable panic. You should also moderate your behavior, as previous plagues suggest. If you're traveling to West Africa as a trained healthcare worker, that will help. If you're going there for just about any other reason, you might want to reconsider (another way in which you can help). But seriously, the fight in West Africa will win or lose the ultimate contest, everyone agrees.

Be aware of your surroundings, maintain good hygiene, remain calm and stay informed. Since this virus mutates and is as aggressive as it is, new information will be coming in often, changing the complexion of the situation. This book will be updated with significant advances, so you may consider borrowing it at least once a year (for free) from the Kindle Library. This will help you stay on top of this ever-changing situation, which is more than half the battle.

It's true that Ebola knows how to survive. Now, so do you.

BANKSY KNOWS: Street Art

Table of Contents

INTRODUCTION

GRAFFITI History of graffiti, some graffiti terms, little known graffiti facts, graffiti's illegality

STREET ART Techniques, Bristol, Dadaism, Minimalism, Surrealism, Expressionism, Pop Art, Andy Warhol, The AAA

BANKSY Banksy Timeline, other contemporary Street Artists, other reclusive artists, the future of Street Art

CONCLUSION

EXCERPTS Samples of other Blujesto Press books

INTRODUCTION

There's not much we can say for certain that we know about the British Street Artist Banksy. Part of his allure (a necessary part for legal purposes) is that his face and true identity are unknown to the public (or any but a rarified few). But we can certainly know more about his work, and about the artistic traditions which have made his work possible. That's the purpose of this book, to put the present day phenomenon in a historical perspective, so as to better appreciate and understand it. You may have heard of Banksy, or even walked past a Banksy, without knowing it, much less without knowing Banksy.

At the end of 2014, the popular modern art form called Street Art was still enjoying great popularity, thanks in no small part to the man known as Banksy. So Banksy knows Street Art, perhaps better than anyone else.

But no artist exists in a vacuum, and Banksy and the Street Art movement with which he'll always be identified are just the contemporary manifestation of cultural artistic movements that trace back over a century (some all the way back to the dawn of mankind).

So here is a quick, fact-filled primer of the artistic evolution of the Street Art movement, and of Banksy's place as the movement's leader, and even of the entire movement's future (if indeed it has one).

There's no question that Banksy knows Street Art, and after reading this book, you'll not only know Street Art, you'll Know Banksy.

GRAFFITI

HISTORY OF GRAFFITI

The first graffiti dates as far back as 30,000 BCE. Prehistoric cave paintings are the first forms of graffiti. The practice was also common in the Roman Empire (approx. 400 BCE - approx. 500 CE). Thereafter it was never considered more than vandalism until the second half of the 20th century.

Graffiti is commonly associated with hip hop, the music and the lifestyle, even spinning off the sub-genre called Rock and Roll Graffiti, commonly associated with the punk rock movement of the late 1970s and early 1980s.

In the '60s, graffiti became a form of political expression by activists, and it was also used to mark gang territory. Then it took root on the earliest era of hip hop, and remained a big part of that culture up until the present day.

Competition entered the world of the graffiti artist in the 1960s. The idea was to create more complicated works in shorter periods of time. The sides of subway cars would have to be covered, sometimes from top to bottom, in the brief time during stops. And since police would always be close on their heals, graffiti artists prized speed and stealth and especially anonymity. By the beginning of the '70s, tags were being used as signatures so the increasingly competitive artists could take credit among other artists for their work. Spray paint became common in graffiti around this time, as it was widely and cheaply available.

Graffiti writing became very competitive in the 1970s and a new creativity became a hallmark of graffiti art toward the early 1980s, even while transit authorities maintained security against the recurrence of the medium.

Graffiti artist Lee Quinones and Fab 5 Freddy had a 1977 gallery opening in Rome. For most Europeans (and others outside of New York), this was a first encounter with the art form.

Increased city security, including new security camera technology, made the years between 1985 and 1989 difficult for graffiti artists in New York. The medium became less popular. 1989's Clean Train Movement was New York's attempt to remove graffiti from the subway system. Graffiti artists took refuge in art galleries and their own privately owned studios.

Then a 2001 IBM ad campaign showed people painting a heart, a peace symbol, and a penguin on city sidewalks. Some of them were actually arrested and charged as vandals.

But the mainstream continued to embrace graffiti. Video game design is rife with graffiti. Urban fashion designer Marc Ecko has long been a vigorous advocate of artistic graffiti, referring to it as recent history's most powerful artistic movement.

Keith Haring has done much to bring graffiti to the commercial mainstream. Haring opened his first Pop Shop in the 1980s. The store offered anyone access to the artist's works which were painted on city walls.

In China, Mao Zedong still holds the record for the world;s longest single piece of graffiti. It includes 4,000 characters which criticizes Chinese society and his own personal teachers.

Graffiti in the Middle East is slowly emerging, with pockets of taggers operating in the various emirates of the United Arab Emirates, in Israel and in Iran. The most famous artist in Iran is A1one, he works in Tehran walls. The religious reference "נ נח נחמ נחמן מאומן" is seen quite commonly graffitied around the holy city of Israel.

SOME GRAFFITI TERMS

- Pissing: Filling a fire extinguisher with paint.

- Throw-Up (aka Bombing): Quick painting with only two or three colors. Crudeness replaces artistic detail in favor of quickness.

- Piece: An elaborate signature, usually the artist's name, usually very stylized and colorful.

- Wildstyle:, Graffiti using connecting points and interlocking letters.

GRAFFITI'S ILLEGALITY

Graffiti often has a reputation as part of a subculture that rebels against authority, giving it much in common with some of the great art movements in the first half of the 20th century. Between 1970 to 1980 the London Underground was covered by messages that were clearly anti-war, anarchist, feminist and anti-consumerist.

And Graffiti has never been legal. In fact, the more popular it became, the more vigorous was the authoritative response.

Philadelphia created PAGN in 1984 with an eye toward combating that city's gang-related graffiti. The city's murals were protected by fines for defacement under this campaign.

In 1995, New York Mayor Rudolph Giuliani created one of U.S. history's most sweeping anti-graffiti campaigns. In the shops was Sale of spray paint was to minors, but the age was changed from 18 to 21 years in 2006.

The University of Sydney's Camperdown Campus features a great example, the so-called Graffiti Tunnel. Tough Australian graffiti laws prescribe fines of up to a $26,000 and up to two years in prison.

STREET ART

In the late 1990s, a new (non gang-related) form of graffiti appeared. More artistic than criminal, this graffiti incorporated stencils, stickers, posters, even sculpture. The internet christened it Street Art, and it became popular quickly and retains its popularity today.

Street Art includes any art developed in public places (generally in the street), and mainly done in an illegal way. The term refers to "graffiti" and some other artistic expression forms in the street.

Street Art includes graffiti artwork, sticker art, stencil graffiti, sticker art, street poster art, sculpture, flash mobs, large installations, and virtually any manner of item or object.

Street Artists generally impart political, emotional, personal, or humanitarian messages into their work. Because street art is basically vandalism as far as the law is concerned, a lot of great street artists prefer to do it anonymously. A lot of artists and citizens consider it little more than vandalism as well, and many in the art community do not consider it legitimate art.

Street Art and Guerrilla Art mean basically the same thing, and certainly they refer to the same movement. The terms' origins are obvious. Street Art takes place in the streets, on the subway cars and the walls of public buildings. It can also refer to anything that can be seen in a public place, artistic installations in locations such as Disneyland. The term Guerrilla Art comes from the manner in which the art is applied. These artists, like the guerrilla rebel armies for whom they are named, appear suddenly out of hiding, strike quickly and fiercely, then fade back into the night before the State's forces can run them down. And this was (and remains) very much the case in Bristol and other cities where Street Art is practiced. The laws are stringently against them, and enforcement is an ongoing concern for city and state governments.

But the two elements work together, and in the world of Street Art they are part and parcel of the same thing. Let us say that Street Art uses guerrilla tactics, I position that will bare out later in this study. But we'll be using the term Street Art instead of Guerrilla Art from here on.

New York, Bristol, London, Berlin, Barcelona, Toronto, and São Paulo are key cities for the development of Street Art.

TECHNIQUES

Graffiti, currently with aerosol cans, is the most common street art technique. But it's by no means the only technique:

Mosaic tiling: Wall art that was popular in Ancient Greece, this wall/floor/ceiling art is comprised by numerous small pieces of colored stone, glass, or other materials. The small pieces work to create a single, larger image.

Murals: Artwork painted onto a wall or a ceiling. Usually quite large, a mural is a single piece, not a painted portion of a larger piece.

Stencil art: Stencils protect a certain portion of a painted surface. The areas left unprotected form words or images. This is a very quick way to apply graffiti, even quicker when combined with aerosol spray can paint.

Sticker art: Images or message displayed on stickers applied to public surfaces.

Wheatpaste: Papering posters to public walls using wheatpaste, a vegetable-starch-and-water based adhesive liquid.

Woodblocking: Artwork is painted on plywood or other cheap material. The wood is then bolted onto street signs for permanence.

Yarn bombing: Uses knitted cloth to decorate other objects, such as wooden boards.

LED Art: It's an art form based on light-emitting diodes. You can purchase them in a cheap way.

BRISTOL: STREET ART'S GROUND ZERO

Bristol is a British city in South West England, west of London. With roughly 1,006,600 citizens, Bristol is England's sixth most populated city (and the UK's eighth most populated). It's the center of employment, education, and culture in South West England.

Recently the economy has become dependent on the electronics creative media, and aerospace industries. The city center docks were recently given a facelift and refitted as a new center of culture and heritage.

So Bristol became the central point for the birth of the Street Art graffiti movement. It had all the cultural and artistic activity, and the hardscrabble urban challenges to inspire inexpensive and outlandish forms of art. Further, Bristol's proximity to the Zurich birthplace of Dadaism and the French birthplace of the surrealist movements, both very influential on street art.

This the city that made Banksy, and it a lot of ways, this is the city Banksy made. Today, Street Art is one of Bristol's principle tourist attractions. Banksy walking tours are among the most popular of several Street Art walking tours.

Let's take a look at some of the artistic traditions which made Street Art possible. These movements produced some of the most evocative and recognizable art of the entire 20th century.

DADAISM

Dada was an artistic and literary movement that started in Europe when World War I was going on. Artists, writers, and intellectuals, from Germany and France, fled WWI and went to Switzerland, where they vented their rage against the war. But not being artists, they turned to nonconventional means of artistic expression. The works included everyday objects, puns, humor, even some obscenities. Marcel Duchamp's copy of the Mona Lisa, upon which he painted a mustache and wrote obscenities, is a classic of this school.

Here's a checklist of elements common to Dada art. Many of these recur when street art rises to the fore over half a century later.

- Dada began in Europe (Zurich) and it soon became an international cultural rage.

- Dada had an antiestablishment nature which didn't follow any of the rules of traditional art, from subject to technique to presentation.

- In its literature as well as its visual pieces, Dada sought to insight emotional reaction, often outrage or shock.

- Dada art does not follow the rules of logic any more so than the rules of art, geometry, or other visual considerations. It is often nonsensical, expressionistic or abstract.

- Dadaism is a multimedia type of visual art, combining various materials, words, and other nontraditional items.

- Dadaism influenced later art movements, including surrealism, constructivism, and street art.

- The movement spread across Europe and over the Atlantic Ocean to New York City.

- Protest combined with whimsey, satire with sarcasm, in the best of the Dadaist movement, and these influences are also apparent in many modern art movements, particularly street art.

CUBISM

Cubism represented a burst of modernism in contemporary art and is crucial to the later development of Street Art. Artists Pablo Picasso and Georges Braque were leaders of the movement. The movement has been described as having two stages: Analytic and synthetic Cubism.

Analytic Cubism represents modern art's sharpest break from traditional types of representation. Here, there was no perspective at all (a staple of art since the Renaissance). Small planes, tilted and shaded, in shallow space, comprised images of human figures.

Synthetic Cubism included cloth materials and other foreign objects. The use of newspapers indicated a political leaning to the movement, but a very abstract and detached expression of it.

Piet Mondrian kept exploring this us a grid, its use of the grid, its shallow space, abstract system of signs.

MINIMALISM

This long-running movement enjoyed three 20th century decades in the spotlight, from the '50s through the '70s. Works in this school are as simple in content as in form, at the expense of personal expression. This later became a staple of the Street Art ethos. Without complex themes, viewers could enjoy a composition more quickly and more intensely. The movement was heavily influenced by 18th century artist Goethe's Alatar of Good Fortune, which was no more than a cube with a stone sphere. In the '20s artists like Duchamp and Malevich created pieces along these lines. As Street Art would later do, Minimalism (and Conceptual Art too) had an impersonal attitude. Simple installations, stark canvases and minimalist sculptures are the hallmarks of the movement, by the likes of Dan Flavin, Donald Judd, Carl Andre and Ellsworth. The late-career work of Henri Matisse, which came to typify the jazz era's artistic ethos, is classic Minimalism, even eschewing lines themselves and only representing the colored spaces (that would have been) within them. With striking imagery which communicates quickly and effectively without being personal, Matisse's work in Minimalism is critical to the development of Street Art.

SURREALISM

The Surrealist Movement, founded in Paris in 1924, sought to unlock the imagination's hidden power by channeling the unconscious. Rejecting literary realism and intellectual rationalism, while retaining a strong influence of Dr. Sigmund Freud, Surrealists held that the conscious mind could repress the imagination's hidden power of the imagination. Taboos weigh the imagination down, according to the surrealists, shattering those taboos released the psyche's power to pierce hidden truths, reveal contradictions, and even inspire revolution. This focus on the imagination places the surrealists in the Romantic tradition.

Surrealists Salvador Dalí and Man Ray were major influences on avant garde artists. And their commercial work (including advertising, film, and fashion photography) brought the Surrealist vision to mainstream audiences. They also heavily influenced later schools, such as Pop Art and Street Art.

And, like later artists like Banksy, this multimedia movement included literature as well as other visual elements.

EXPRESSIONISM

Abstract Expressionism began in 1940s New York. Its use of universal themes and profound emotion and universal themes were influenced by Surrealism and accented with the era's general post-war anxiety. For the first time, New York artists usurped their Parisian counterparts as leaders of the art world.

Sculptors like David Smith, and photographers such as Aaron Siskind, joined the movement, making it another multimedia movement, inspiring the other similar movements to follow (among them Street Art).

POP ART

A reaction to, and an expansion of, the Expressionist movement, Pop Art challenged tradition and traditional approaches and media. Pop Art's central conceit is that there is no difference between icons of popular culture, and art, the two are combined as one.

Pop Music was central to Pop Art too, and figured heavily into the movement's multimedia installations. The work is generally ironic and impersonal, like much of what appears in the later Street Art movement.

Pop Art began in the 1950s, but hit its stride in the '60s. Jasper Johns, Roy Lichtenstein and especially Andy Warhol typified the movement and the commercial ethos behind it. Lichtenstein's comic book-inspired pieces, including word bubbles, are classics of the movement and remain popular today. The further co-mingling of art and advertising and use of striking imagery that could be quickly absorbed and digested make this movement the most closely related to Street Art, both chronologically and intellectually.

ANDY WARHOL

Perhaps more than any other single artist, Andy Warhol shares much with Banksy, and was a significant contributor to the traditions in which Banksy later worked, and in which he still works today. Warhol is, in many ways, the stepping stone between the Dadaist movement and the Street Art movement. Bur really, few artists or videographers of any stripe can get away without tipping their hat to this daring visionary.

Warhol graduated from the Carnegie Institute of Technology in 1949. His major was pictorial design. Right after college, Warhol moved to New York straight out of college. His work in advertising includes ads for I. Miller, Christmas cards for Tiffany & Co. among various album and book covers.

In 1960, pop art was a revolutionary style of art which started in 1950s England (in other words, the birth of the Street Art movement). Everyday items were popular subjects in both schools of art.

Warhol started with comic strips and Coke bottles, until a friend suggested he paint his two favorite things. Among them were money and a can of soup.

Warhol's famous Campbell's soup cans appeared in his first exhibition, at the Ferus Gallery in Los Angeles, 1962. in an art gallery came in 1962 at the Ferus Gallery in Los Angeles. He displayed his canvases of Campbell's soup, one canvas for each of the 32 types of Campbell's soup. He sold all exhibits paintings as a set (one for each of the 32 flavors of the line's soup) for a $1,000, a lot of money at the time.

Warhol discovered silk screening in 1962, which enabled him to produce his imagery fast enough to keep up with demand. The process is like stenciling, only silk is used instead of paper. Multiple versions of a single image could be created this way, and it became a hallmark of Warhol's late-career style, found famously in his paintings of Marilyn Monroe.

Warhol kept painting through the 1960s, and made nearly 60 movies between 1963 and 1968. Most were very experimental films, such as Sleep, a nearly six-hour film of a sleeping man.

Warhol survived an assassination attempt on July 3, 1968, being declared clinically dead for a brief period during doctor's attempts to revive him. His health never fully recovered.

During the 1970s and 1980s, Warhol continued to paint in the '70s and '80s, but focused his attention of publishing Interview magazine and several pop art books. Warhol dabbled in television as well. He also began publishing a magazine called Interview and several books about himself and pop art. He even dabbled in television. He died after gallbladder surgery on February 21, 1987.

THE AAA

No, not that AAA. This AAA (often called The Triple A) were Stanford students who exposed to LSD experiments among a 1960s community of intellectuals and artists. New music and video helped the AAA form a psychedelic rock band which tried to expand the viewers' (and creators') consciousness. They often opened for San Francisco's the Grateful Dead and they even headlined at Ken Kesey's legendary Acid Test Graduation. Strobe lights and film projections were the hallmarks of their long, improvisatory performances. Consciousness expansion and the artistic lifestyle led the collective to Colorado. Lars Kampman, the AAA's leader, died of AIDS in the 1980s and the collective disbanded. Survivors and friends sometimes reunite on the Colorado land the collective owns. The AAA combined political and satirical perspectives with sense-dazzling visuals, a lesson that was not lost on Banksy or his contemporaries.

BANKSY

Who is Banksy?

Banksy's identity is technically unknown, but there are theories. Worthy candidates include Bristol native Robin Gunningham. Gunningham is said to have been an artistic student, and reportedly worked with stencils.

One of the few people to have interviewed Banksy in person, the Guardian's Simon Hattenstone, reported that Banksy wore a T-shirt and jeans to their meeting, in addition to wearing a silver chain, a silver earring ... and a silver tooth.

Banksy denies being is Gunningham, who was born in 1973. As if to prove his point, Banksy created a type of self-portrait which features Gunningham.

Here's what we do know, or think we know, about the elusive, anonymous artist.

BANKSY TIMELINE

It's believed Banksy was born in Yate, near Bristol, in 1974 or 1975, but he grew up in Bristol. He is between 28 and 35 years old and he began to paint in Bristol between 1992 and 1994.

Banksy first appeared on the graffiti scene in the early 1990s and was associated with Bristol's DryBreadZ Crew (DBZ).

Banksy himself has said that he attempted to paint bubble letters on a public train when he was 18 years old. On the run from police, Banksy hid under a garbage truck and was inspired by stenciled letters on the bottom of the truck.

Banksy moved to London by 2000. He stayed with friends Jamie Eastman and Luke Egan. The record label where Eastman worked used a few of Banksy's works, and his pieces began appearing in the area.

In 2002, Banksy's Existencilism, his first international exhibition, held at L.A.'s 33?. It was quickly followed by the 2003 exhibit, London's Turf Wars, was held in an East London warehouse. Cattle painted with faces, and various commercial motifs, highlighted the exhibition. Animal activists protested even though the exhibit was meant to raise awareness of animal cruelty and exploitation.

Banksy depicted Queen Victoria in an explicit Lesbian position. Pop singer Christina Aguilera bought the original print for £25,000. Banksy's variations of famous works by Andy Warhol, Edward Hopper, Monet, and Leonardo da Vinci.

Banksy of England £10 notes were distributed at the popular Notting Hill Reading Festival and at the Carnival. The notes, featuring the head of Lady Diana and not legal tender, fetched hundreds of pounds on ebay.

Banksy traveled to the West Bank and Palestine in 2005. There he stenciled images (nine of them) on the historic and revered Bethlehem Wall. These works showed children playing and digging, an armored dove carrying an olive branch,a ladder ascending the wall itself, a girl frisking a soldier, and others. A second Los Angeles exhibit followed, Barely Legal. The three-day exhibit was highlighted by a gaudy and gold-trimmed pink elephant in the room, a symbol of the specter of world poverty.

Banksy's prints of Kate Moss, the famous British model Kate Moss, recreated the style of the late Andy Warhol. They sold at Sotheby's for £50,400 (five times the estimated figures). The same auction saw a record-setting £57,600-sale of a stenciled image of the famous Mona Lisa, but with paint dripping sadly from her eyes.

Banksy's auction prices are astronomical: Bombing Middle England sold for £102,000, Balloon Girl sold for £37,200, and Bomb Hugger sold for £31,200. Numerous other works also garnished incredible amounts. Ballerina with Action Man Parts sold for £96,000, Glory sold for £72,000, and Untitled (2004) sold for £33,600. Space Girl & Bird set a record for the artist's work when it sold for £288,000 at Bonhams of London in 2007.

In Norfolk, a £1,000 mobile home that Banksy doodled on ten years before sold for a startling £500,000.

Banksy's major installations and collective exhibits include Banksy's Stonehenge. Featured at the Glastonbury Festival, the piece was comprised of portable toilets. Another of Banksy's most iconic pieces is a battered and crumpled phone booth, stabbed with an ax, dripping blood, lying on its side. It appeared in 2006 on a street in Soho and was quickly hauled away by officials.

Banksy's 2008, Cans Festival featured almost 40 international guerrilla Street Artists, including Blek le Rat and others. The show, named for the famous Cannes Film Festival, was held in an abandoned tunnel.

Banksy's first official New York exhibition opened at the Village Pet Store and Charcoal Grill in early October. One animatronic animal display featured a mother hen tending to her McNugget chicks as they pecked at containers of dipping sauce.

A post-Katrina New Orleans was the location of a spat of Banksy originals, many featuring his famous rats and various human subjects. A boy swinging on a rescue tube and looters entering windows were well-placed in the crumbling Lower 9th Ward. A hooded KKK member hanging at the end of a noose, and a man sitting in a rocking chair under a no loitering sign, were two other images that were promptly covered.

In 2005, Banksy placed paintings in various prominent New York museums, including the Met, the Museum of Modern Art, the American Museum of Natural History, and the Brooklyn Museum. In London's British Museum, Banksy hung a replica of a prehistoric cave painting which depicted a hunter-gatherer pushing a shopping cart. The piece was reportedly destroyed.

Banksy's work transcended the visual image and took a multimedia turn In 2006. The mischievous guerrilla artist replaced 500 copies of the first CD by celebritart Paris Hilton's with a mix of songs by rock band Danger Mouse, with titles such as "What Have I Done" and "Why Am I Famous?" When the switch became known, copies were pulled (but not before a few copies managed to be sold by some lucky collectors). Extant copies have fetched up to£750 online. Bansky also placed an inflatable doll wearing the uniform of a Guantanamo prisoner in the Disneyland theme park in California.

Banksy stenciled animal's thoughts as art at the London and the Bristol Zoos. Another of his recent victories was a set of pieces which commemorated the London Olympics of 2012. The Olympic series depicted, among other images, a pole vaulter clearing a barbed-wire fence to land on what seems to be an abandoned mattress. A javelin thrower who aims not a javelin but a surface missile, is another image from the series, highlighting a nearby military installation meant to guard the Olympic site.

Despite Banksy's fame, or perhaps because of it, property owners, city officials, and (most unfortunately) fellow street artists commonly (and quickly) destroy his work almost as quickly as it goes up. One Melbourne,

Australia piece was destroyed, despite being protected behind a sheet of Plexiglas.

Seven Banksy works in Toronto were destroyed. One in Detroit was excavated by an art group bent on preserving the piece. His pieces are quickly covered even in his home country. One Muslim community center painted over an image on their building. A parachuting rat in Australia was accidentally destroyed by a team of unfortunate plumbers in the 1990s.

In 2009, the Banksy vs. Bristol Museum show featured 100 unique pieces which included large installations and animatronic displays. Upwards of 300,000 visitors clamored to attend the exhibition.

The Banksy film, 2010's Exit Through the Gift Shop was nominated for an Academy Award. Before the Sundance Film Festival premiere, Banksy created almost a dozen pieces in Utah's Salt Lake City and Park City. Sundance has shown films by unknown artists but never an anonymous one. In this film, Banksy turned the tables on the only man to film him. He created a remarkable documentary which was as much personal journey as it is an exposé of modern the art world. Banksy has also published six books which feature his opinions, perspectives, and, of course, his art. Wall and Piece (Random House, 2005) and Banksy: You Are an Acceptable Level of Threat (2012) are popular.

The HBO documentary BANSKI HITS NEW YORK was released at the end of 2014, at the time of this book's publication.

Banksy's works have appeared worldwide: America, Australia, Canada, England, France, Israel, Jamaica and Palestine. Banksy's works and message transcend art, politics, philosophy and satire.

Banksy is quite well-known, but no artist exists in a vacuum. He inspired other artists, and he's been inspired by other artists; some of his strongest inspirations were classical artists and others contemporary street artists. Massive Attack's 3D is one of his recognized inspirations, as is Frenchman Blek le Rat. known as the father of stencil graffiti. Blek has publicly challenged Banksy as a copycat. Banksy evinces no tension toward le Rat and recognizes that the Frenchman's work often resembles and predates his own.

OTHER CONTEMPORARY STREET ARTISTS

1. KASHINK: Paris-based Kashink is a graffiti artist specializing in male figures, usually hairy, fat, bespectacled men dressed as shaman, gangsters or other dubious or mysterious male archetypes.

2. Miss Van: Barcelona-based, French-born artist Van is truly one of the pioneering females in the medium of street art. Baroque-era figures in period dress and even masquerade masks, exuding sexuality and erotic danger.

3. Clare Rojas: San Francisco-based Rojas visual folktales which challenge traditional gender roles. Recently, her work developed from being more homey to being more abstract and geometric.

4. Lady Pink: Ecuador-born and New York-raised Lady Pink started painting subway cars in 1979. Her first solo exhibition ran when she was just 21, and she dominated the female-artist niche for years without knowing it.

5. Maya Hayuk: Brooklyn-based muralist Hayuk is known for a geometric, psychedelic approach, in addition to Ukrainian influences crafts into her psychedelic and geometric visions.

6. Olek: Master of crochet Olek, based in New York and born in Poland, constantly transforms new spaces, people and objects. Politics, pop culture and the punk ethos combine to create crocheted pieces artworks.

7. Lady Aiko: Tokyo-born Lady Aiko is based in New York. She utilizes elements of graffiti, abstraction, Pop Art, and traditional Japanese images.

8. Faith47: A South African, Faith47's textured images juxtapose nature and spiritual themes against the background of urban environs.

9. Shamsia Hassani: Hassani is one of Afghanistan's first female graffiti artists. Her work incorporates burqa and other elements unusual in western art. Women's struggles in Afghanistan are among her central themes.

10. Alice Mizrahi: Mizrahi creates empowering and emotive images of girls and women as sacred archetypes. She co-founded Yonite, (with artist Tootfly).

11. Bambi: Bambi is a female street artist many have called the female Banksy. Celebrities such as Amy Winehouse, Kim Kardashian, and Cara Delevingne, are among her favored subjects, a fascination she shares with the late Warhol.

Not only is Banksi not the first or only so-called Street Artist, he's not the first reclusive artist either. In fact, he's the latest in a long line of famous and in some cases infamous people.

OTHER RECLUSIVE ARTISTS

1. J.D. Salinger

The epitome of the reclusive, publicity shy artist, author J.D. Salinger spent much of his life in seclusion. Salinger became famous in 1951 with The Catcher in the Rye, still among the 20th century's most widely read, studied, and beloved books. Salinger released a short story collection and a second novel, Franny and Zooey, then retired to Cornish, New Hampshire. Salinger blocked a Swedish publisher's unauthorized, unofficial sequel to The Catcher in the Rye. Perhaps the most extraordinary thing about Salinger's reclusiveness is that by all accounts he has never stopped writing. He wrote steadily, reportedly for his own pleasure. The specter of numerous unpublished Salinger manuscripts (one per year, some say) has been a constant source of speculation by fans and scholars. Salinger died at age 91 in 2010.

2. Greta Garbo

Swedish actress Greta Garbo was quite famous in both the silent film era and afterward. The star of Flesh and the Devil and Anna Christie worked less and less, until finally retiring in 1941. Garbo became just as well-known for withdrawing from the public eye entirely. She became a New York City legend and a whole grail for paparazzi.

3. Thomas Pynchon

Gravity's Rainbow author Thomas Pynchon has refused to make a public appearance or grant an interview since the early seventies. One famous theory about Pynchon, suggested by a California newspaper, proposed that Pynchon was the assumed name of famed recluse J.D. Salinger. Pynchon denies this. No recent photos exist, but CNN did capture Pynchon on film in the late 1990s. Pynchon himself appealed to the station not to air the footage. Even when appearing on popular primetime series The Simpsons, which he's done twice, his character is seen with a bag over his head.

4. Syd Barrett

Syd Barrett was so reclusive that many people assumed he died years before he actually did (in 2006). The founding member of British rock band Pink Floyd became senile from overuse of psychedelic drugs (which may or may not have antagonized underlying psychological defects). He spent much of his life, and all of its second half, at his family home in Cambridge, painting and gardening.

5. Stanley Kubrick

Hollywood film director Kubrick delivered several film classics, including 2001: A Space Odyssey, A Clockwork Orange, and Full Metal Jacket. A reported fear of flying led him to work out of his secluded England manner. Although reclusive, he is not unseen (like Pynchon or Salinger). British conman Alan Conway presented himself as the reclusive director until the director's death in 1999.

6. Emily Dickinson

Among America's great poets, Dickinson was notoriously reclusive, rarely leaving her home (or even her bedroom). Dickinson spent almost all her life in her family home until her 1886 death by suicide. She reportedly only spoke to visitors from behind the closed front door. Only a very few of her poems were published in her lifetime. When she died at the age 55, her sister Lavinia discovered a trunk spilling over with over 1,800 poems. Lavinia succeeded in getting the poems published in1890. Dickinson's work has not fallen out of print since then. She remains among the 1800s' most celebrated literary figures, and a favorite of gloomy teenage girls everywhere.

7. Harper Lee

Lee's To Kill a Mockingbird is one of the greatest and most commonly studied novels of the 20th century. The book was published in 1960 to immediate acclaim, but Lee virtually vanished from publishing. In 2007 she accepted the Presidential Medal of Freedom, though she remains largely reclusive.

8. Bill Watterson

Cartoonist Bill Watterson's strip Calvin and Hobbes was always publicity shy. After his retirement in 1995, he withdrew entirely from public life. With most requests to license his characters' likenesses turned down, even they seem to have become recluses.

9. Terrence Malick

Days of Heaven director Terrance Malick is a Harvard graduate as well as a former Rhodes scholar. Malick's peak came in the 1970s, and he returned to film directing in the late 1990s. Said to be currently working on a new film (perhaps even a trilogy), he still will not release any photos of himself and has made very few appearances. It seems unlikely he will resurface, even to support his new work.

10. Cormac McCarthy

Cormac McCarthy, author of All the Pretty Horses, is among the most reclusive figures in contemporary literature. Nobody in the literary world knows what McCarthy looks like, much less where he lives. He refuses interviews and speaking engagements. After brief and surprising appearances at the Academy Awards and on the Oprah Winfrey Show, McCarthy once more receded into the shadows.

Although not great artists, honorable mention should also go to these notorious recluses: Chess master Bobby Fischer, late industrial millionaire Howard Hughes, even late ex-Beatle John Lennon.

THE FUTURE OF STREET ART

As we have seen, Street Art it at the pinnacle of its popularity. At the time of this publishing, November of 2014, it may even have begun to fall from this peak. And whatever one thinks of the artfulness of the movement, there can be no question that the future of the art form is very much in doubt.

Street Art is in a long line of art forms which rebel against popular notions of what art is. Since Street Art has been embraced by that same mainstream audience which determines those popular notions, Street Art has in many ways rung its own death knoll. It has become the very thing it was designed to rebel against, a fact that is unavoidable to future Street Artists, especially in this irony-heavy medium.

Graffiti walls are disappearing, and penalties are escalating. The great popularity of the medium once again becomes the author of its own demise in this way as well. As more people do it, authorities step up their efforts against it.

So the streets themselves are less and less hospitable to Street Artists. The likely results are that this kind of artwork will go more and more to the internet for expression. The internet is the perfect way to distribute multimedia artworks and to advertise installations. In fact, the exodus of Street Art from the street to the internet has already begun. The problem with that, of course, is that multimedia art produced for the internet is no longer Street Art (as it isn't primarily seen on the street). It's also not guerrilla art, because the pressures of time and antagonism are no longer present. Instead of appearing, striking and then disappearing into seclusion, internet artists can take their time, create in private, and then distribute online at their leisure. There isn't very much that's guerrilla about it.

It's also important to remember that Street Art is an art movement (those who prize it believe it to be). And so it must necessarily share the same life cycle that every artistic cycle has: It is influenced by a previous movement or movements, it enjoys a period of underground popularity, it is recognized by the popular culture to an extent, it influences the next group of artists, then is replaced by the movement which it influenced as is marginalized. Every movement leading up to Street Art has had this life cycle.

Street Art is currently at the end of its own life cycle. With Banksy, the movement reached its last two periods, mainstream recognition and influence. So it seems historically certain that the next thing for Street Art is that it will be marginalized in favor of the next art wave, currently being shaped by Street Art's influence. Precisely what that will be, nobody can know for sure and it's even hard to estimate. We'll just have to watch and wait.

That's not say that Street Art will disappear. Its place in that long line of artistic movements insures that those same recurring elements will continue to recur, but they will do so at the hands of other artists, likely using new and different media. That's the nature of art; it always has been and it always will be.

CONCLUSION

Banksy knows Street Art. He knows Warhol, he knows Dadaism. He knows the temporary nature of the type of work he does, and how much that lends to its satirical nature. He knows that anonymity can become part of the artist's work as much as part of his identity. He knows Street Art.

And know, so do you.

And though Street Art is undoubtedly on the wane, it's not dead yet. And as long as Banksy continues to create publicly (which seems likely and is certainly possible for decades to come), the specter of Street Art will linger. And as that story develops, this book will be updated to reflect new developments in the art form, and in the career of this amazing personality. So consider returning to the Kindle Library or use your Amazon Prime subscription to read updated editions absolutely free. Now you'll know Banksy, you'll know Street Art, and you'll keep knowing them!

YELLOWSTONE KNOWS: Impending Doom

Table of Contents

INTRODUCTION

VOLCANIC HISTORY Plate tectonics theory, principle types of volcanoes, calderas, the six supervolcanoes, the Toba eruption, the Yellowstone caldera eruptions, the greatest volcano eruptions in history

YELLOWSTONE Yellowstone facts, other signs of impending disaster, reasons not to worry, the melting roads

GLOBAL WARMING AND VOLCANIC ACTIVITY

OTHER THREATS OF IMPENDING DOOM Extra-terrestrial threats, natural disasters, tsunamis, heat waves, U.S. earthquakes and related tsunamis, the aftermath of Fukushima, Ebola

CONCLUSION

EXCERPTS Samples of other Blujesto Press books

INTRODUCTION

Yellowstone National Park knows impending doom, it knows it all too well. This caldera is one of the world's few active so-called supervolcanoes, and it's located practically right in the center of North America. Experts agree that an eruption from this sleeping giant would virtually wipe out most of life on that continent, and throw the entire globe into economic and ecological chaos. The recovery of the human race from such an event is uncertain, at best. Some would consider it the end of the human's reign on Earth without question.

What's more, because Yellowstone is such a volatile place geologically, and because the planet itself is in the throws of severe and detrimental global changes, there is more activity there now than at any time in recorded history.

This makes Yellowstone a kind of geographic litmus test, a way to gage what kind of other changes are happening, and which are likely to happen in the near future.

But controversy surrounds Yellowstone. Some say the danger is minimal and some say there's no real threat at all. Some insist that a catastrophic eruption is not only likely but inevitable, and that it may happen sooner rather than later. But everyone agrees that there are fascinating secrets to be revealed at the heart of the Yellowstone caldera, and a wealth of information that can be extracted from it. What we do with that information will be our own responsibility as a race. We cannot predict volcano eruptions, but we can forecast them to a degree, and only the right information will allow us to do that.

So we present the best, most-current information on the ever-changing face of Yellowstone, from fire-breathing monster to benevolent protector. We'll put the caldera in a historical perspective, and compare it with other possible threats to the human race, to help you better prepare for what yet may come. Yellowstone may not be the source of impending doom, or it may be; but Yellowstone surely does know impending doom. And now, so will you.

VOLCANIC HISTORY Plate tectonics theory, principle types of volcanoes, calderas, the six supervolcanoes, the Toba eruption, the Yellowstone caldera eruptions, the greatest volcano eruptions in history

Plate Tectonics THEORY

Plate Tectonics is a now-accepted view of the Earth's surface as being fragmented, a collection of shifting plates or slabs. They average 50 miles or so in thickness. The plates, which comprise the Earth's crust, ride a hotter, deeper, more fluid and therefore mobile zone (the mantle) beneath. The plates are believed to move several inches every year. The majority of Earth's still-active volcanoes can be found near or along these boundaries between the shifting plates. They're known as plate-boundary volcanoes. But some currently active volcanoes are not linked to plate boundaries at all, and quite a few of those intra-plate volcanoes form linear chains in oceanic plates. The famous Hawaiian Islands are the most well-known example of this type of volcanic chain, as it developed when the northwest-moving Pacific plate passed over a so-called hot spot which initiates the generation of magma and also the volcano formation process. The Pacific Ocean Basin's peripheral areas contain the boundaries of numerous plates. They are peppered by many numerous volcanoes which form the infamous Ring of Fire. The Ring offers superb examples of these plate boundary volcanoes, including the state of Washington's Mount St. Helens.

PRINCIPLE TYPES OF VOLCANOES

Volcanoes fall into four general types: Cinder cones, shield volcanoes, composite volcanoes, and lava domes.

CINDER CONES

These are the simplest volcanoes. Cinder cones are comprised of particles and hunks of hardened lava which were all ejected from one singular vent. The oval or circular cone is formed after gas-charged lava is blasted into the air, then crumbled into smaller fragments which become solid and fall as cinders around the vent. Cinder cones are notable for bowl-shaped craters at their summits and they rarely rise to more than one thousand feet above the surrounding surface. These volcanoes are plentiful in the western United States and throughout Earth's other volcanic regions.

In 1943 a Mexican cinder cone erupted, sending cinders to fall back and create a cone of roughly 1,200 feet in height. The remaining molten rock poured out in lava flows. This is the process of most cinder cone volcanoes: Gas eruption, cone formation, lava flow.

COMPOSITE VOLCANOES

Composite volcanoes, also sometimes called stratovolcanoes, are some of Earth's grandest mountains. These symmetrical, steep-sided cones are very large and are built on layers of lava flow, cinders, volcanic ash, bombs, and blocks. They can reach 8,000 feet in height. Japan's Mount Fuji, Ecuador's Mount Cotopaxi, Californian's Mount Shasta, Oregon's Mount Hood, and Washington's Mount Rainier and Mount St. Helens represent this type of volcano.

Composite volcanoes generally have craters at their summits which contain a main vent or vents clustered together. Lava flows through breaks in the wall of the crater or through cracks on the cone. Lava becomes solidified in these fissures, forming dikes which act like ribs and greatly strengthen the integrity of the cone.

A composite volcano can form a reservoir deep in the Earth's crust which then rises to the surface. This type of volcano is built by the accumulation of earthen material ejected during an eruption. It gets larger as the material builds up over time. Dormancy of a composite volcano, on the other hand, leads to erosion, exposing hardened magma.

Crater Lake in Oregon is a variation of this type of volcano. A series of huge explosions roughly 7,000 years ago threw out volumes of ash flows and avalanches. Lava quickly drained from the weakening upper mountain, which collapsed and formed a large depression. When that depression filled with water, it became Crater Lake. The lake's Wizard Island is a tiny cinder cone which rose up during the volcano's last gasp. Depressions like these are often steep-walled, large, and basin-shaped. They represent the collapse of large areas over and around volcanic vents. These calderas range in size and form. Sometimes they're vaguely circular and between one and 15 miles wide; sometimes they're massive depressions which are often elongated and as long as 60 miles.

SHIELD VOLCANOES

Shield volcanoes consist almost entirely of once- and current fluid lava flows. Sequential flows pour in every direction from a single, central summit (or sometimes a group of vents). They build a broad, sloping cone, generally a flattened shape. The profile can resemble a warrior's shield, giving this type of volcano its name. The liquid lava called basalt lava spreads quickly and widely, then cools in thin sheets. Lava also leaks from fractures in the vents and develop on the zone's flanks. Many of the shield volcanoes in Oregon and Northern California boast diameters of 3 to 4 miles or more, with heights of up to 1,500 to 2,000 feet. The famous Hawaiian Islands are comprised of linear chains of these types of volcanoes, including Kilauea and Mauna Loa on the big island of Hawaii. They're currently two of Earth's most active volcanoes. The ocean floor there exceeds 15,000 feet. Mauna Loa is the largest of the shield volcanoes (and it's also Earth's largest currently active volcano). It stands 13,677 feet high, 28,000 or more feet above the depths of the ocean floor.

Basaltic lava may pour quietly out of the long fissures instead of from the central vents. It may flood any countryside with flow after flow, lava forming broad plateaus. These lava plateaus can be found in Iceland, eastern Oregon, southeastern Washington, and southern Idaho. Along Idaho's Snake River, and the Columbia River in Oregon and Washington, lava flows of this type are exposed and may measure more than one mile in their total thickness.

LAVA DOMES

Lava domes are formed by bulbous but small masses of lava too heavy to flow any reasonable distance. A dome typically grows from internal expansion, fed by a volcanic vent. The surface cools, hardening, before shattering and spilling fragments. Sometimes a dome will form craggy knobs or even spines over, near or around the vent. Others form coulees, which are short, steep lava flows. They usually appear in the craters, sometimes on the volcano's flanks. Novarupta Dome was formed during the 1912 Katmai volcano eruption (in Alaska). It measures 200 feet tall and 800 feet wide. Lesser Antilles, Mont Pelée in Martinique, as well as California's Mono and Lassen Peak domes are lava domes.

CALDERAS

Think of calderas as extreme volcanoes ... they're often called supervolcanoes, in fact. These are by far the most destructive volcanoes due to the manner in which they are created. Shaped like an inverse volcano, a huge chamber of magma bulges under the ground due to the enormous temperatures of trapped natural gasses. Circular cracks form from the magma chamber outward toward the surface. These rings act as relief valves of a sort, allowing magma to harmlessly escape. Once the pressure is relieved through an eruption, the ground caves in and leaves a huge depression. These types of volcanoes are the world's largest and most dangerous, with some measuring between 15 and 100 kilometers in width.

THE SIX SUPERVOLCANOES

A supervolcano can shower red-hot debris and molten rocks over incredible distances. Any eruption of this magnitude could fill Earth's atmosphere with sulfuric acid, ash, and sulfur dioxide. It could potentially cause another Ice Age (and has caused Ice Ages in the past). The Volcanic Explosivity Index (VEI) measures volcanic eruptions, a scale which goes from 0-8, 0 representing non-explosive and 8 representing a supervolcano eruption.

Yellowstone National Park happens to sit on perhaps the largest active subterranean chamber of molten rock (a caldera). The magma chamber is not very far below the Earth's surface, and it fuels the various volcanic attractions for which Yellowstone National Park is so justly famous. Yellowstone's last major eruption was roughly 640,000 years ago. It ejected roughly 8,000 times the quantity of ash and lava as the eruption of Mount St. Helens. The Yellowstone volcano is alive and very well today.

Second to Yellowstone (in the pantheon of North America's calderas) is the Long Valley caldera. The caldera is 200 square miles in total size, located near the Nevada state line, not far south of Mono Lake. Long Valley's biggest eruption was roughly 760,000 years ago, and it spilled 2,000 to 3,000 times as much molten lava and hot ash as Washington's Mount St. Helens. Afterward, the caldera floor dropped down about a mile, a U.S. Geological Survey revealed. Ash drifted as far away as Nebraska. A cluster of strong 1980 earthquakes, in addition to the 10-inch rise of much of the caldera's floor, still worries experts. In the early 1990s, carbon dioxide from huge amounts of magma from below started to seep through the ground, killing trees in the mountain areas around the caldera. These are signs of trouble to come.

The Valles caldera forms a 175-mile pock right in the center of northern New Mexico, just west of the city of Santa Fe. The caldera exploded over 1 million years ago, accumulating 150 or so cubic miles of blasting ash and rock as far as Iowa. As is the case with other calderas, there are signs of heat and that means activity. Hot springs are common and active around Valles.

Indonesia's Toba caldera was created over 74,000 years ago. Toba ejected many thousands of times more material than Mount St. Helens released in 1980. Some researchers believe Toba's ancient eruption and the mini Ice Age it triggered influenced the development of the human genome, which suggests that every living human descends from just a few thousand survivors of some catastrophic event roughly 10,000 years ago.

Taupo caldera in New Zealand has been filled by water, creating one of Earth's most picturesque landscapes. The lake was created by a huge eruption roughly 26,500 years ago. But the 485-square-mile caldera is far from dormant. It erupted in 181 CE, sending materials up to 22 cubic miles by contemporary accounts.

One of the most recently troubling calderas in the world is the 150-square-mile Aira caldera, near Kagoshima in southern Japan. The 150 square-mile volcano erupted 22,000 years ago, belching out 14 cubic miles of volcanic debris. Much of Kagoshima Bay was formed during this event, which is comparable in size to roughly 50 Mount St. Helens eruptions combined ... and is still considered active.

A massive caldera eruption has not happened in recorded history. There are no human witnesses and no recorded observations of such an event. But all evidence suggests that these eruptions have altered the course of life on this planet, and a comparable event may yet end it.

THE TOBA ERUPTION

This eruption ejected up to 6,000 km3 of pulverized rock and magma and enough sulfur gases to form over 5,000 megatons of sulfuric acid aerosols into the stratosphere. This created a volcanic winter which lasted for several years. The drop in temperatures wiped out vegetation and almost crippled the food chain which was dependent upon it, humans included.

THE YELLOWSTONE CALDERA ERUPTIONS

Wyoming's Yellowstone National Park is a mecca for tourists and vacationers hoping to appreciate the rugged beauty of the area. Its mysterious and consistent volcanic activity is also a big draw. Over the last half-century, scientists have studied the area, hoping to be able predict what it will do in the future.

Experts estimate that some 2.1 million years ago, the first of three huge caldera-forming eruptions rocked the area. The subsequent two eruptions happened after periods of roughly 600,00 to 800,00 years. The Yellowstone Caldera last erupted roughly 640,000 years ago.

These three caldera-forming eruptions were (respectively) 2,500, 280, and 1,000 times more powerful than the 1980 Mount St. Helens eruption. Taken together, those three caldera-forming eruptions expelled sufficient lava and ash to actually fill up the entire Grand Canyon. There was enough ash and volcanic debris ejected from those eruptions to cloak the western half of the United States in roughly four-feet of ash. 600 or so cubic miles of debris filled the atmosphere.

Most caldera-forming volcanoes are found over subducting tectonic plates, but the Yellowstone Caldera is fed by a hot spot beneath the crust. This explains how volcanic activity occurs in the central area of tectonic plates, far from the much-more geologically active margins of the plates.

A huge magma chamber roughly 40 by 80 kilometers lies beneath the Yellowstone Caldera. The ground there is bulging dramatically upward, indicating that the magma chamber is once more on the move. As there is no historical precedent for an eruption of this type, scientists can't predict if a giant eruption will happen again. But they know that the Yellowstone eruptions were far more powerful and much more violent than the Toba eruption.

Before we take a closer look at Yellowstone, let's take a look at some of the most violent and costly eruptions in history.

GREATEST VOLCANO ERUPTIONS IN HISTORY

Siberian Traps, Siberia:

The collectively known Siberian Traps is the deadliest volcano Earth has ever known. The worst mass extinction in the history of our planet was caused by the Permian era eruption of the traps, roughly a quarter-billion years ago. Only 10 percent of life on Earth survived. It sent greenhouse gases by the billions of tons into the atmosphere. Thanks to the catastrophic global warming which followed, life on Earth took millions of years to recover.

Tambora, Indonesia:

This colossal 1815 eruption produced an ash cloud that was so big, the season of summer simply didn't happen in either Europe or North America in 1816. 70,000 and 90,000 lives were lost, making this the deadliest eruption in human history.

Santorini, Greece:

Santorini, a group of five islands, was originally one island, until Krakatau blasted the entire island roughly 3,600 years ago. Ash deposits were roughly 100 feet thick and have been found as far as 19 miles in every direction. Legends of the lost city of Atlantis are born of this eruption, which is said to have destroyed the ancient civilization. More concretely, the eruption marked the beginning of the end of the Minoans on the island nation of Crete.

Krakatau, Indonesia:

In 1883, Indonesia endured a caldera-forming eruption (Yellowstone was formed from such a cluster of eruptions). It released roughly 200 megatons of explosive power. The biggest nuclear bomb ever detonated was still only one quarter as powerful as this eruption. 100-foot-high tsunamis and flows of scalding ash washed ashore upwards of 25 miles away. Since then, a series of lesser eruptions has begun creating a new island in the void of the old volcano.

Mauna Kea, Hawaii, USA:

Hawaiian volcanoes produce low-viscosity basalt that oozes and flows like a river. Over time, these flows slowly build mountainous structures. This volcano, almost five thousand years dormant, began erupting enough to create a nearly 34,000-foot high mountain (from its base underwater).

Grimsvotn, Iceland:

A volcano buried underneath the Vatnajokull glacier in eastern Iceland called Grimsvotn last erupted in 2004. It showered huge amounts of liquid called Jokulhlaupsm, resulting in floods that were catastrophic.

Mount St. Helens, Washington, USA:

By May 18, 1980, the nearly 10,000-foot mountain had swollen to the point of bursting, which it finally did on that Sunday morning. It was the most deadly volcanic eruption in the history of the United States, resulting in 57 lives lost and nearly $3 billion in damages.

Ontong-Java Plateau, South Pacific:

125 million years ago, this volcano erupted and the basalt covered a region of the Pacific Ocean about the size of Alaska. It was as thick as 30 kilometers in some places. Amazingly, this single eruption is believed to have lasted six million years! This is what scientists call a large igneous province (LIP). They form when vast amounts of hot molten magma rise up from perhaps thousands of miles in the mantle, still not far from Earth's core.

Scientists disagree as to whether these LIPs seep up in massive sheets or erupt in mighty explosions. Mass extinctions, however, seem to happen in close proximity to these eruptions, none of which have happened in recorded history.

YELLOWSTONE

Yellowstone's thermal basins originate deep inside the earth, where the planet's core is surrounded by the viscous mantle, above which is the planet's crust. The so-called hot spot creates the incredible heat which is anchored in the mantle. This is the same hot spot which is responsible for maintaining volcanic activity scattered across southeast Idaho, and that includes the Craters of the Moon National Monument. After movement over millions of years, the planet's crust has now placed this hot spot directly under Yellowstone.

Roughly 600 thousand years ago, the hot spot sent a hot column of magma to the surface, which formed the massive magma chamber. The chamber filled and it pushed up against the crust of the Earth, creating a huge dome.

Pressure against the surface formed cracks along the dome's edge. A tremendous eruption expelled a huge amount of hot magma, which emptied a massive portion of the chamber. That evacuation caused the dome to collapse in what is generally believed to be among the planet's most violent explosions ever.

The next 500,000 years saw gradual lava flow filling much of the crater. And this is the active area which provides heat for Yellowstone's thermal attractions, such as the famous Old Faithful geyser.

The three massive eruptions over the last 2.1 million years released enormous amounts of magma, pumice, ash and gas into the atmosphere. Rapid evacuation of so much magma caused the ground to collapse. This swallowed the overlying mountains and created several broad, cauldron-shaped depressions or calderas.

The first eruption created the volcanic deposit Huckleberry Ridge Tuff, just south of now-popular Mammoth Hot Springs. This enormous event was one of the largest volcanic eruptions anywhere on the planet, and it formed a caldera which is more than 60 miles across.

The second, smaller eruption happened 1.3 million years ago and formed the Henrys Fork Caldera, which is located near Island Park (west of Yellowstone

National Park). It created the volcanic deposited which today is known as Mesa Falls Tuff.

The most recent and most terrible caldera-forming eruption happened 640,000 years ago and created the 50-mile-long, 35-mile-wide Yellowstone Caldera. Pyroclastic flows left thick deposits now called the Lava Creek Tuff. Volcanic ash was blasted into the atmosphere, while deposits of the ash can be found as far away as Iowa, Louisiana, and California.

Yellowstone's three eruptions happened when massive amounts of rhyolitic magma built up at fairly shallow levels in the planet's crust (just three miles beneath the surface). This thick, sticky magma was highly charged with dissolved natural gas. It moved upward, putting stress on the planet's crust and generating massive earthquakes. Magma approached the surface, pressure decreased, and expanding gas began to cause violent explosions. Rhyolite explosions are responsible for creating many of Earth's calderas, such as the ones found at Katmai National Park in Alaska, which was formed during a 1912 eruption.

The effects of another caldera-forming eruption at Yellowstone would be worldwide. Vast portions of the United States would be buried in ash and debris, and the atmosphere would be so thickly polluted that it would plunge the entire planet into a severe Ice Age, crippling the food chain all over the globe and disrupting global climate as well. The list below describes this impending doom in greater detail.

YELLOWSTONE FACTS

A lot of things about the Yellowstone Caldera are still unknown, but not everything. Here are a few things experts agree on:

- Another Yellowstone eruption seems to be approaching with each year. Since 2004, areas of the national park have risen by up to ten inches.

- The hot spot underneath Yellowstone is approximately 300 miles wide.

- An eruption of Yellowstone could be up to 1,000 times more powerful than the 1980 Mount St. Helens eruption.

- A Yellowstone eruption would spew volcanic ash roughly 25 miles into the air.

- A massive Yellowstone eruption would destroy the entire northwest of the United States.

- A full-scale Yellowstone eruption most certainly would create a volcanic winter that would cool the Earth demonstratively (experts agree that a worldwide 20-degree dip is likely).

- A massive Yellowstone eruption would kill every living thing within a 100 mile radius of the park.

- The United States would never fully return to normalcy after such an eruption, losing perhaps 70% of its inhabitable areas.

- Scientists agree that Yellowstone will most certainly erupt eventually, although there is some controversy as to when that may happen, and how soon that may be.

- A full-scale Yellowstone eruption could deposit a layer of ash up to 10 feet deep or more and up to 1,000 miles away or perhaps even further.

- A Yellowstone of this sort would cover all of the midwestern United States with ash. Food production in the United States would be destroyed in its entirety.

RECENT SEISMIC ACTIVITY IN YELLOWSTONE

One of the key indicators of volcanic activity is seismic activity. And volcanic activity can forewarn the possibility of earthquakes. With that in mind, there has been a lot of seismic activity around Yellowstone which must not go unnoticed by the diligent observer.

In September, 2014, 130 earthquakes hit the Yellowstone area over the course of just a single week. Yellowstone's earthquake clusters started on September 10 and were still shaking until roughly 11:30 a.m. September 16, almost an entire week nonstop!

Yellowstone's reservoir of super-hot viscose rock is at least two-and-a-half times larger than previously believed. The Geological Society of America recently announced that an earthquake which measured 9.0 magnitude (or larger) may result from the expansion of Yellowstone's massive mantle plume expansion.

By most accounts, the supervolcano has been rising at a record-fast rate since as recently as 2004. Its floor has risen three inches per year, and this has occurred over the last three straight years. It's the fastest rate since record-keeping of this type began back in 1923.

REASONS NOT TO WORRY

But this shallow depth is creating changes that are causing a lot of people to worry, perhaps unnecessarily. The fact is that the ground in Yellowstone routinely deforms and swells in various places. Over a period of several months, a six-mile-wide area has risen roughly 1.4 inches and it's moved close to half an inch to the southeast. The U.S. Geological Survey's Yellowstone Volcano Observatory reassures the public that this is a normal circumstance for the area and that they present no real indicators of eminent volcanic activity.

All this activity could actually be beneficial in a lot of ways. Yellowstone's mercurial, quickly changing nature gives geologists a lot of unique opportunities to learn about the current state of Earth's geology, and the history of life on this planet. In fact, an enzyme was found in thermos aquaticus, a type of bacteria, plentiful in the water. It went on to play a significant part in the advancement of new DNA-studying technologies. The enzyme was subsequently used in everything from DNA fingerprinting to AIDS diagnosis; an entire billion-dollar industry that found life in the waters of Yellowstone National Park.

Other research has revealed how helium moves under the Earth, and that improves our understanding of underground reservoirs and of natural gas.

Dozens of scientists continue to monitor the volcano, tracking the quantity and quality of earthquakes in the area and recording changes in the Earth's surface. In mid-February of 2014, the ground of Norris Junction was 3.5

centimeters higher than normal for five full months, which still doesn't compel most experts toward panic.

THE MELTING ROADS

In July, 2014, popular Firehole Lake Drive, a 3.3-mile road through Yellowstone National Park, was shut down when the asphalt started to melt. The road transported visitors to many of the popular thermal attractions including Great Fountain Geyser, Firehole Lake and White Dome Geyser. The same heat which propels the water of the geysers, the hot spot, was responsible for the damage to the roads. Increased summer heat also played a part in making the road impassable. Continued earthquakes and acidic residue in watery sprays from the geysers did additional yearly damage. Hikers and motorists were asked to avoid the areas. All roads were re-opened within a week or so, and experts agreed that this was not a sign of an impending eruption.

GLOBAL WARMING AND VOLCANIC ACTIVITY

By the 1990s, two decades or so of rapid global warming came to the attention of experts and scientists, yet they predicted no substantial change in that trend in the years to come. Despite the rise those decades saw in the emission of greenhouse gases, the Earth's surface temperature remained fairly stable. How could this be? Experts turned to the surface of the oceans and the heat being released from the beneath the Earth's crust. Wind patters, among a variety of other forces, were also taken into account.

The contributions of volcanoes on temperatures in the troposphere (the lowest layer of the atmosphere) has surely played a role in keeping the planet cooler.

Huge eruptions release sulphur dioxide into the Earth's atmosphere, sometimes even the stratosphere. There, the gas coverts into volcanic aerosols, which are basically drops of sulphuric acid. These aerosols deflect sunlight and reduce Earth's atmosphere's temperature.

This volcanic aerosol has increased in the stratosphere during the opening years of the 21st century. So more sunlight is being reflected away from Earth and back into space.

In this way, volcanic activity may actually be combating the same global warming which the human race has been fostering since the industrial age. The pattern we notice regarding atmospheric emissions is this: Greenhouse gases in the atmosphere warm the troposphere beneath it and cool the stratosphere above it. Major volcanic eruptions warm the stratosphere above and cool the troposphere below.

So Volcanoes can certainly impact climate change. But there's another mysterious conflict: During a major explosive eruption, massive amounts of natural gas, aerosol drop, and volcanic ash are thrown up into the stratosphere. The ash then falls rapidly (within several days to weeks) and can have little longterm impact on climate change. Volcanic gases (sulfur dioxide among them) may be the cause of global cooling. On the other hand, volcanic carbon dioxide (a known greenhouse gas) may have the opposite effect, promoting global warming.

Although sulfur dioxide from contemporary eruptions has sometimes been known to cause global cooling of the troposphere and lower atmosphere, carbon dioxide from volcanic releases has never been known to cause global warming at either level. However, this is likely due to the limited amounts of carbon dioxide which were released during the period of contemporary volcanism. They have simply been of insufficient magnitude to produce any global warming. It has often been suggested that some intense volcanic releases of carbon dioxide far back in the Earth's past may have caused some global warming (and may even have caused some mass extinctions). However, this remains a subject of considerable scientific debate and likely will for some time.

In fact, research indicates that humans currently release more deadly CO_2 into the air than active volcanoes do.

But global warming surely has an effect on volcanism everywhere on the planet, although it may not be for the same reasons most people would think.

The fact is, a hotter planet will have increased volcanic surface activity, and here's why:

When the Earth's climate is generally warmer, as it is now, glaciers melt fairly quickly, raising sea levels. This means the weight on the continents decreases while the weight on the oceanic plates increases, altering the quality and quantity of stresses on the Earth's crust. This can change where and when magma may find open routes to the surface. So periods of global warming increases volcanic activity (and the Earth is in such a period now, few people doubt).

And since the Earth cools more slowly than it heats, those changes are less dramatic and so cause less stress upon the Earth's crust. Therefore there is less volcanic activity during periods of cooling on the planet.

The impact from man-made warming is still unclear, so shorter-term historical variations must be studied in order to ascertain a clearer view of what to expect in the near future.

But experts still insist that Yellowstone is unlikely to be the history-shattering eruption that some expect. There are other, more grave threats to life on Earth, other sources of impending doom. To ignore them in favor of worrying about Yellowstone, some would say, is to miss important information and to be willfully ignorant. But that's not you, or you wouldn't be reading this book. So read on ...

OTHER THREATS OF IMPENDING DOOM

EXTRA-TERRESTRIAL THREATS

Though the chances of Earth being hit by an extinction-event-sized meteor are considered very slim, there are other extra-terrestrial threats, some of them from within our own solar system.

A nearby hypernova, which results from the destruction of a sufficiently large star, may hit our planet with sufficient gamma radiation to wipe out Earth's protective ozone layer, exposing the planet and its inhabitants to solar radiation in deadly amounts.

Rogue star Gliese 710, an orange dwarf, may enter the Milky Way galaxy as soon as 1 - 2 million years from now, presenting possibilities for collision and perhaps planetary destruction.

Even Solaris (the Earth's own sun) poses a significant threat to life on Earth. In approximately 8 billion years, our solar system's sun will have burned through the very last of its gaseous fuel supply. At this point it will swell, becoming what astronomers call a red giant. The sun's increasing diameter will ultimately encompass our planet's current orbit and Earth will be vaporized. But long before that happens, Solaris' gradual expansion will increase Earth's temperatures, boiling the oceans and creating a desert planet. Once the sun's mass has decreased (unlike its size), Earth could be released from its gravitational pull. In this scenario, the planet will be too far from the sun to be incinerated, though the planet's oceans will surely freeze. Even so, some life may continue near the planet's remaining hydrothermal vents along the ocean floors, thanks to plate tectonics and volcanic activity.

NATURAL DISASTERS

Between 1980 and 2007, climate-related natural disasters (such as heat waves) affected 98% of all people affected by all natural disasters (non-climate oriented events like earthquakes). 2009's economic losses to natural disasters were roughly $63 billion. In 2010, the figure had climbed to $222 billion. In 2009, about 15,000 people died from natural disasters, but in the 2010, the figure was roughly 320,000. In 2010, Latin American natural disasters took 300,000 lives, damaged $49.4 billion in damage. Forest fires and a heat wave claimed roughly 15,000 Russian lives alone.

Some experts estimate that by 2015, on average over 375 million people per year are likely to be affected by a climate-related disaster, over 50% more than in the previous decade.

Geographers at the University of South Carolina estimated the likelihood of dying from the most common deadly natural hazards.

- coastal 2.3
- mass movement 0.9
- winter weather 18.1
- wildfire .4
- tornado 11.6
- severe weather 18.8
- lightning 11.3
- geophysical 1.5
- flooding 14.0
- heat / drought 19.6
- hurricane / tropical storm 1.5

TSUNAMIS

There's a Caribbean fault line, the Septentrional fault, which is known to have generated numerous deadly tsunamis. Such a tsunami today could affect upwards of 35 million individuals, according to scientists. Virtually every inhabited coastline on Earth is vulnerable to tsunami.

HEAT WAVES

Excessive temperatures take more U.S. lives than any other natural disaster. Meanwhile, global temperatures are increasing, summer seasons are getting longer, power systems are being worn down and are strained to the point of malfunction. People are also living longer, and the aged are among the most prone to death during heat waves. All this means deaths from heat waves are likely to increase.

U.S. EARTHQUAKES AND RELATED TSUNAMIS

Two hundred years ago, three magnitude-8 earthquakes rocked the Midwestern United States. Since then, the region has become heavily populated, but building codes in the area were never meant to accommodate seismic activity, which is inevitable. The damage there will be catastrophic if another big quake hits.

A Southern California earthquake of sufficient size could create a tsunami which may do upwards of $42 billion in damages. It would hit with such speed that most coastal residents would be trapped with no chance to evacuate. The area would sustain incredible damage from the quake itself as well.

Another huge North American earthquake would wreak havoc on its local area. And an even worse threat (much worse) would be the tsunami which may result, originating from a fault line which is identical to the fault line which caused the 2004 Indonesian tsunami.

Also worthy of note; 2011 saw a leap in the seismic quality and quantity of earthquakes worldwide.

Earthquake cluster in January, 2011:
January 1: 7.0 magnitude, Santiago del Estero in Chile
January 2: 7.1 magnitude, off the coast of central Chile
January 12: 6.0 magnitude, off the coast of central Chile
January 18: 6.5 magnitude, Japan's Bonin Islands
January 18: 7.2 magnitude, Pakistan

The disastrous Japanese earthquake and tsunami were only the indicators of a new and dangerous phase of seismic activity. In 2015, Japan is expecting several catastrophic earthquakes with magnitudes of 8 or higher.

Volcanic activity is on the rise beyond Yellowstone, including Mexico's Popocatepetl volcano, which registered 39 so-called exhalations in a single 24-hour period. Ash wafted as high as three miles above the Sakurajima volcano in the southern city of Kagoshima, forming a plume roughly 3 miles high. Lava flowed beyond the half-mile mark while massive rocks rolled blindly down the mountain. It was Sakurajima's 500th eruption during that year alone.

THE AFTERMATH OF FUKUSHIMA

Fukushima Dai-Ichi station is owned and operated by the Tokyo Electric Power Company (9501). In March 2011, an earthquake and tsunami caused the meltdown of three reactors. Roughly 300 metric tons of contaminated groundwater seeped into the Pacific Ocean every single day. Those figures came from the Japanese government, which may or not have been telling the whole story. This was the worst nuclear accident since Chernobyl.

And it's still a huge problem!

From May 2011 to August 2013, upwards of 10 trillion becquerels of strontium-90, 20 trillion becquerels of cesium-137, and 40 trillion becquerels of tritium were released into the Pacific Ocean. Cesium isotopes emit flesh-penetrating gamma rays, and they are perhaps the most dangerous radionuclides emitted by the entire plant. The radioactivity in plant wastewater comes from inadvertent contact between the isotopes and cooling water pumped through nuclear plants. South Korea has already banned imports of fish from Japan's northern Pacific coast.

However, scientists found low levels of the radioactive material Iodine-131 in Pacific Ocean waters between Orange County to the south and the Palos Verdes Peninsula to the north. Iodine is commonly used to diagnose and treat thyroid cancers. But since the Ports of Los Angeles and Long Beach are where the most concentrated amounts were found, officials believe that the iodine may be originating from the Terminal Island Water Reclamation Plant nearby.

At the same time, current levels of radiation in the world's oceans are leading radiologists and oceanographers to deem most concerns unwarranted.

Experts report that any water exposed to radiation from the Fukushima plant would reach the United States at levels at perhaps 100 times lower than the country's drinking water safety threshold, according to the Nuclear Regulatory Commission. Fukushima radiation is being erroneously blamed for everything from sea-lion deaths to sickened polar bears, according to a Canada's Times Colonist editorial.

It's not all good news in the aftermath of Fukushima, however. The European Committee on Radiation Risk (ECRR) has reported that radioactive emissions from Fukushima 1 may cause a widespread surge in cancer cases. Of the 3 million people living within 100 kilometers from the nuclear plant, experts predict that roughly 200,000 will contract some form of cancer.

EBOLA

By November of 2014, the date of publication of this book's first edition, Ebola Hemorrhagic Fever had taken roughly 5,000 lives, become pandemic in three West African countries and invaded countries as disparate as the United States and several European nations. Though not an airborne virus, over 50% of those who catch the disease die from it within a few weeks. The death, from organ failure due to fluid (i.e. blood) loss, is horrific.

The United States Public Health Institute has predicted that potentially 1.4 million individuals may become infected by the Ebola virus by January 2015 if it continues unchecked. A group of European security officials issued a declaration that the Ebola virus epidemic ought to be treated in the same way as the threat posed by nuclear weapons.

CONCLUSION

Yellowstone knows imminent doom, although it may appear to be a less likely candidate to bring said doom than various other factors that may yet destroy the human race at virtually any time.

But because Yellowstone is such a geographically active place, it can be a good way to read our planet, when considered with other factors. And though a Yellowstone eruption may not occur, related natural disasters such as earthquakes surely can (and do and will) and that could have serious implications on potential for a life-threatening eruption from the famous and infamous North American supervolcano.

But Earthquakes and eruptions (of this sort) cannot be predicted, they can only be forecast. Armed with an understanding of the forces at work in, on, and around the planet, you'll be better able to forecast natural disasters such as these. And these are the ones that count.

Yellowstone knows imminent doom; and now, so do you.

NIKOLA TESLA KNOWS: How to Invent the Future

Table of Contents

INTRODUCTION

BEFORE TESLA Archimedes, Leonardo di Vinci, Benjamin Franklin, Thomas Edison

TESLA Nikola Tesla, inventions, ideas, little-known facts

AFTER TELSA The computer revolution, Tesla Motors

CONCLUSION

EXCERPTS from other KNOWS books and several Blujesto Press books.

INTRODUCTION

Distance, Tesla hoped, would be overcome in word, action and thought. Humanity would be united, he theorized, war would be rendered impossible and world peace would reign. For Tesla, abundant and affordable energy was the base of a peaceful co-existence among the diverse human race.

If this sounds like a quaint notion from a century ago, you'd be right and wrong. It is a century-old idea, but it's no quaint notion, it's an absolute fact. It's the internet, and all the telecommunications technology it relies upon. and Nikola Tesla not only envisioned it but helped to create it, from the ground up.

Relegated to the dustbin of history for too long, Tesla's contributions can no longer be denied. And even more than the enormous legacy of his rival, Thomas Edison, Tesla's work continues to shape the future.

Tesla surely knows how to invent the future; not only did he invent his future, he invented ours.

So here's the volume which gives you the facts about Tesla you need to know, putting the newly restored reputation of this nearly forgotten genius in historical perspective. We'll take a look at the inventors who made Tesla's work possible , and those who benefit most from it. This is a fast-paced, fact-filled book that spares you the excessive scientific jargon to give you a quick and thorough understanding of this man's amazing innovations, in his time and ours.

Tesla knows how to invent the future, and now, you'll know Tesla.

BEFORE TESLA Archimedes, Leonardo di Vinci, Benjamin Franklin, Thomas Edison

When asked how if felt to be the world's smartest man, Albert Einstein replied, "You'll have to ask Nikola Tesla." And while Einstein and Tesla were contemporaries, and fellow geniuses, they weren't fellow inventors. Einstein was a physicist and a scientist.

But Tesla did not invent in a vacuum. In fact he is one in a series of likeminded inventors dating back to the ancients. In order to understand Tesla's work, one must know the names and deeds of those who paved the way for him, and who influenced him most and had the most in common with Tesla and his vision.

ARCHIMEDES

Some of the greatest inventions in the world were made by Archimedes, during his 3rd century BCE lifetime. These inventions were very simple in functionality and even the theories he came up with were extremely logical. Archimedes had made most of his inventions when he was living in Syracuse.

Archimedes is best known for the screw that bears his name. This hydraulic screw raised water from a lower to a higher level. Originally designed to pump water from leaking boats, the long screw housed in a pipe in used in many inventions today.

Archimedes discovered that any object immersed in liquid displaces some of that liquid. The amount of displaced liquid would equal the weight of that object. Archimedes principle, as it's called, laid the foundation for countless inventions that would follow.

He invented the magnifying glass, though it was much larger originally than it us now. It was intended to be a fire-starting device, an activity for which it is still used today.

One of his greatest inventions is the catapult, designed to protect Syracuse from deadly Roman invasion.

LEONARDO DI VINCI

The 15th century's Leonardo di Vinci is best known as the pre-imminent Renaissance Man and perhaps the greatest painter of all time. But his inventions were often the prime focus of his work.

Leonardo di Vinci invented the ball bearing, which now used in countless inventions today, including computers, airplanes, electrical generators and many, many more. Though many believe Philip Vaughan invented the ball bearing in 1794, but Leonardo's designs for the very same invention predate his patent by almost 300 years. Di Vinci also designed the roller bearing and the needle bearing.

One of the cornerstones of all invention, the exploded view of a machine when drawn. Virtually no other inventions could have been fully realized without this design development technique.

OTHER DI VINCI ORIGINAL DESIGNS INCLUDE:

- Tank

- Helicopter

- SCUBA diving gear

- Autonomous robots

- Continuously variable transmission

Di Vinci discovered plaque on the walls of veins 400 years before modern science named it arteriosclerosis.

Di Vinci discovered Newton's Third Law of Motion (that a force is either a push or a pull which acts upon any object as a result of its interaction with any other object) a full 200 years before Newton was even born!

Di Vinci had notions of plate-tectonics and evolution hundreds of years before these theories were introduced to the scientific mainstream.

BENJAMIN FRANKLIN

Colonial genius and founding father Benjamin Franklin was a writer, a statesman, a publisher, and perhaps first and foremost an inventor until close to the end of his life in 1790. His contributions were very much in the same tradition as Tesla's, and the others' in this study.

BEN FRANKLIN INVENTED:

- Franklin/Pennsylvania stove

- Lightning rod

- Flexible catheter

- 24-hour, three-wheel clock

- Glass armonica, a musical instrument made of spinning glass

- Bifocals

- The long arm (which was an extension arm to facilitate the removal of books from off of high shelves)

FRANKLIN FOUNDED OR CO-FOUNDED:

- The Library Company of Philadelphia, which was America's first circulating library

- Union Fire Company, which was America's first volunteer fire department

- The American Philosophical Society, America's first learned society

- America's first liberal arts academy, Pennsylvania Academy & College, the first American liberal arts academy and which is now the University of Pennsylvania

- Pennsylvania Hospital, American's first public hospital

- The Philadelphia Contributorship, America's first mutual insurance company

BENJAMIN FRANKLIN WAS THE FIRST TO:

- Describe electricity using the words negative and positive

- Create a political cartoon in America

- Serve as Ambassador of the United States

- Chart the Gulf Stream's currents and temperatures and currents between the U.S. Atlantic coast and the UK and Western Europe.

- Introduce colonists to Swiss Barley, Scotch Kale, Chinese kohlrabi and rhubarb

FRANKLIN'S OTHER ACHIEVEMENTS:

Franklin discovered that electricity (lightning) existed in storm clouds.

Franklin suggested that the colonies join together in a confederation, known as the Albany Plan of 1734. It was never adopted.

Franklin also suggested the concept of Daylight Savings Time.

Franklin improved street lamps, enabling them to give more light and making them more difficult to vandalize.

Franklin also first noted that prolonged exposure to lead would cause sickness.

Franklin surmised that the germs associated with the common cold were passed between individuals through indoor air.

THOMAS EDISON

The turn of the (20th) century's Thomas Edison is the most well-known inventor in the world, and a key player in the story of Nikola Tesla. Edison has become, quite literally, the first word in electrical lighting. But as part of the world which created Tesla and which Tesla created, Edison made several notable contributions to the modern world.

THE PHONOGRAPH

The phonograph had two needles: one for playback and one for recording. Voices spoken into the mouthpiece were indented into a cylinder by the needle. The other needle would read those indentations.

It now seems likely that Edison kept tinkering with his phonograph until the end of 1877, even if the actual date of completion is often cited as August 12. The patent was filed on December 24th, 1877. President Ruthorford B. Hayes invited Edison to the White House to demonstrate the machine.

The Edison Speaking Phonograph Company was established in 1878 to sell the new phonograph.   He also suggested various other uses for this machine, including:

- dictation and letter writing
- audio books for blind people
- recording family members to keep a family record, or audio "home movies"
- clocks that announce the time
- music boxes and toys
- telephone connections to record communications

ELECTRICITY AND THE LIGHTBULB

Edison didn't actually invent the lightbulb. But he did improve the then-half-century-old idea. Edison used a small carbonized filament, lower current electricity, and an improved vacuum inside the globe. Thus Edison produced a practical, reliable, long-lasting light source in 1879. Edison wound up inventing the incandescent electric light and also a safe, practical electric lighting system.

Most of the attention on the early light bulb was fixed on the discovery of the right filament. But Edison had to invent no fewer than seven separate system elements, including:

- an improved dynamo
- a durable light bulb
- the parallel circuit
- devices to maintain constant voltage
- the underground conductor network,
- light sockets fitted with on/off switches
- insulating materials and safety fuses

The first public demonstration of Edison's incandescent lighting was given in December 1879, when Edison electrically lit the Menlo Park laboratory complex.

The electric utility industry evolved from gas and electric carbon-arc commercial and street lighting systems. In the late 1880s, power demand for electric motors brought the industry to around-the-clock service. Transportation and industry needs also drove up the need for service. Small central stations peppered many U.S. cities buy the end of the 1880s. Electricity spread worldwide, and so did Edison's electric light, as well as his reputation. His electric companies thrived, and were eventually collected as Edison General Electric. In 1892, EGE merged with Thompson-Houston and the company became General Electric.

MOTION PICTURES

Thomas Edison filed a caveat with the Patents Office on October 17, 1888, which described a device that would record and reproduce objects in motion, the kinetoscope.

Eastman Kodak started to supply motion picture film stock, which made allowed Edison to increase production of new movies. Edison built a New Jersey production studio. Its roof opened to utilize daylight. In fact, the entire building could be moved to catch the sun's rays.

Inventors of the Vitascope asked Edison if he could supply film and even manufacture the film projector itself under the Edison banner. The Edison Company developed a projector of its own, the Projectoscope, at which point it no longer marketed the Vitascope. The first motion pictures were shown in American cinema movie houses on April 23, 1896, in New York City.

TESLA Nikola Tesla, inventions, ideas, little-known facts

NIKOLA TESLA

Nikola Tesla is said to have been born precisely at midnight, July 9th/10th 1856, to the Serbian Smiljan, Lika family, subjects of the Austria/Hungarian Empire.

Nikola was born the second son of Djuka Mandic and the Reverend Milutin Tesla, well respected Serbian Orhodox priest. In 1863, Tesla's brother Daniel was killed in a riding accident. The shock of the loss unsettled the young Tesla. The boy who reported seeing visions, early signs of his lifelong mental illnesses. Tesla arrived in the United States in 1884 to enter the employ of non other than Thomas Edison. He became a U.S. citizen in 1891. After winning the War of the Currents against Edison in 1891 with his demonstration of wireless communication, Tesla was regarded as America's premier electrical engineer. Tesla lacked comparable skills handling his finances, however, and he died forgotten and impoverished at age 86.

Electrical power was developing rapidly toward the end of the 19th century. 1882 saw the first commercial power plants. They used direct power currents, however, which were limited in their distribution area. However, the AC power system was their to correct that need and transmit high-voltage power over tremendous distances.

INVENTIONS

THE TESLA COIL AND TRANSFORMER

The Tesla Coil resulted from experiments with high voltage and high energy. Little more than a grounded spiral wire with a HV power supply and a spark gap, it's still being used as a component in countless electronics. The first Tesla Coil patent was issued in 1891.

ALTERNATING CURRENT MOTORS AND TRANSFORMERS

By the end of 1887, Tesla had filed for seven U.S. patents which fully described the alternating current system of motors, generators, transmission lines, transformers and lighting.

Tesla's discovery of the rotating magnetic field is one of his great achievements. The field was produced by when two and three phase alternating currents interact in a motor winding. Tesla's induction motor and polyphase system for the generation and transmission of electricity was born of this rotating magnetic field discovery. Colossal amounts of electric power could be generated and then transmitted efficiently over incredible distances.

In 1888, Pittsburgh's Westinghouse Electric Company bought Tesla's patent rights to his polyphase system of alternating-current (AC) dynamos, motors, and transformers. The price was $25,000 in cash, $50,000 in notes and aper-household royalty of $2.50 for every motor.

Thus began a struggle for dominance between Edison and his direct-current systems on one side, and the Tesla-Westinghouse alternating-current system on the other. Tesla-Westinghouse eventually won out. Around that time, the Edison Company was taken over by financier J.P. Morgan who combined it with other companies and formed the General Electric Company. Both companies offered competing bids to supply power to the upcoming Chicago World's fair, which would then be the first fully electrically lighted fair in history. GE wanted to utilize the DC system while Tesla-Westinghouse bid to do it with a new AC system – for nearly half of what GE proposed.

The Tesla-Westinghouse AC system won, and the Chicago World Fair opened on May 1, 1893, when the US president Grover Cleveland pushed a button and the "electric" future began in the most spectacular lighting display.

Tesla demonstrated the rotating magnetic field principle with the Egg of Columbus as well as the first neon lights. Tesla wrote the names of his favorite scientists in the twisted neon tubes.

NIAGARA FALLS

Tesla didn't invent Niagara Falls, of course. But he dreamed of harnessing the falls's power, and in October of 1893 Westinghouse was awarded a contract to build the power plant at the falls. Further more, they'd be using Tesla-designed generators. Those were 5000 horsepower generators, the largest such machines of that time. General Electric licensed several of Tesla's patents, was awarded a contract to build 22 miles of transmission lines to Buffalo, a city near the Niagara Falls.

Among 13 patents that were used by Westinghouse Company for the Niagara Falls Power Station, nine were Tesla's patents.

Tesla held nine of the 13 patents utilized in the Niagara Falls Power Station. Tesla's polyphase system, in fact, is still used to generate and transmit electricity. And it's Tesla's three-phase and split phase motor systems which make the conversion of electricity into mechanical power possible.

Thomas Edison is believed by many to have brought electricity to common use in the United States. But Edison was a master at promoting himself, and the companies and foundations named for him continue that tradition. But Edison, of course, did not create the alternating current system; in fact he was against it and tried to slander its uses as dangerous. Edison even went so far as to invent the electric chair to demonstrate (and demonize) the current's danger.

But Nikola Tesla discovered the rotating magnetic field principle in 1882; he patented it in 1888 and that's what gave our society its modern system of electric power distribution.

RADIO

Because Guglielmo Marconi may have been the first to send a message all the way across the ocean, he is no doubt partly responsible for the development of radio. But it was Tesla who actually invented it.

The theoretical basis of electro-magnetism was described by James Maxwell. Heinrich Hertz tested Maxwell's theory in 1878 through 1888, verifying the existence of radio waves via his highly successful experiments from 1878-88. Today's radios do not use the appartus used by Marconi and Hertz. Tesla's basic radio patent applications were filed in 1897. They were granted in 1900.

1943: The United States Supreme Court's landmark decision settled the dispute between Tesla and Guglielmo Marconi, Marconi Wireless Telegraph Company of America vs. United States. The court rendered Marconi's basic patent No.763,772 dated June 28 1904, to be invalid, 1904. Tesla's March 20, 1900 patent No. 645,576, and its subdivision patent dated May 15, 1900 for apparatus No.649,621, had priority. Even so, the International Telecommunication Union did not mention Tesla in its 100 Year of Radio special journal issue.

Further, the 1909 Nobel prize in Physics was awarded jointly to: Marconi and Carl Ferdinand Braun in recognition of their contributions to the development of wireless telegraphy.

TERRESTRIAL STATIONARY WAVES

Still one of his greatest achievements. The Earth, he proved, could be a conductor of electrical currents. He insisted the planet was responsive to minute variations in electrical vibrations. The right frequency, Tesla said, would make the Earth ring like a tuning fork. Tesla lighted 200 lamps from 25 miles away without the use of wires. He also created man-made lightning flashes up to 135 feet (41 meters). At a certain point, Tesla was convinced that he'd received pulses from another planet. This claim was generally derided by the scientific community.

Tesla experimented with lighting types of various kinds, also a carbon button lamp, on electrical resonance. To calm fears of AC's safety, Tesla gave visitors demonstrations wherein he allowed electricity to flow through his body.

ROBOTICS AND REMOTE CONTROL

What Tesla called telautomation was actually the foundation of all remote control systems. in 1898 at the first Electrical Exhibition in Madison Square Garden in 1898, Tesla demonstrated how ships and other mechanical gadgets could be remotely controlled via a wireless principle. Tesla believed that all living beings are driven by impulses. So why can't non-living things be so driven, but from external impulses? And so Tesla gave us the essence of the robot. As if foreseeing the danger of artificial intelligence, Tesla warned that human replicas must have inherent limitations, namely in growth and propagation. He envisioned robot companions, intelligent cars, autonomous systems, and the use of sensors. This is the basis for computers and, the ultimate (and some would say inevitable) advent of artificial intelligence. At the time, few could see its many practical applications, even as today life without remote control can hardly be imagined at all.

WIRE POWER

Prior to his wireless power inventions, Tesla patented in 1897 a high frequency system that transmitted power by wire (harmlessly, at long last). Instead of being a circuit, this system is a single wire without a return. It uses Tesla coil configurations at the receiving and the sending ends.

WIRELESS POWER

Tesla recognized that there was only a small difference between broadcasting electrical power and transmitting radio signals. Sending and receiving stations were both tuned to one another by means of tesla coil circuits.

In 1893 Tesla believed that it was practical to use powerful machines to disturb the electrostatic conditions of the earth. In this way, he felt he could transmit intelligible signals and perhaps even power itself According to Tesla, it would not require a great amount of energy to produce a disturbance which might travel all the way around the planet. Tesla's magnifying transmitter was key to that task.

DISK-TURBINE ROTARY ENGINE

Tesla's powerhouse in a hat came in several versions; one was less than a foot in diameter and developed 110 h.p. at 5000 RPM. Tesla believed that larger turbines would hit 1000 HP. The engine runs free of vibration, and it's is cheap to manufacture as only the rotor bearings need to be fitted to close tolerances. The engine also requires very little maintenance. The rotor can be easily replaced, if required. The turbine can run on compressed air, steam, oil, or gasoline.

SPARK-GAP OSCILLATOR

Tesla helped establish the 60 cycle alternating current power system, which is still being used today. But Tesla dreamed of going into millions of cycles.

He discovered that the secret was in the capacitor. With a capacitor circuit, the spark-gap oscillator, he achieved higher frequencies by non-mechanical means.

MANMADE EARTHQUAKE

Tesla's fascination with resonance led him to experiment with it both electrically and mechanically.

Tesla attached a compressed-air vibrating mechanism to a steel pillar. A noticeable quaking started building up, plaster started falling, windows cracked, plumbing burst. The mechanism was operating at the same resonant frequency of the deep sandy subsoil layer under the building, creating a manmade earthquake. Tesla's building shook too, and Tesla destroyed the device.

Tesla also affixed a small, battery-powered vibrating mechanism to a steel girder still under construction. The entire steel framework vibrated, and the earth beneath it did too.

IDEAS

ELECTROTHERAPY

Is this one of Tesla's invention, or an idea, or some combination of both? Imagine an entire branch of medicine is based on the Tesla coil frequency's healing effects. Tesla knew high-frequency vibrations' therapeutic value. Although Tesla never patented anything in this area, he shared his findings with the medical community. Subsequently countless related devices have been patented by others.

Electrotherapy devices were popularly sold through the Sears catalog and ads in popular magazines. Self-treatment was very common. Electrotherapy remains popular, perhaps now more than ever with advances in electronic technology. In sports and chiropractic medicine, low-frequency AC / DC pulses are exercising muscles and relieving pain for an increasing number of patients. High-frequency electrotherapy is enjoying recent popularity as part of holistic and alternative healing regiments. High-frequency therapies are also being investigated as treatment for cancer.

PURE LIGHT

Tesla hoped to create pure light, or cold light, buy generating electric vibrations. It would require vibrations of 350 to 750 billion cycles, and Tesla believed that could be achieved. Full-spectrum lighting of this sort is today believed by some health practitioners actually to have healing properties.

SKY LIGHTING

The widely available Edison filament incandescent lighted up much more brilliantly than they usually might. This is so due to the effects of high frequencies on the rarefied interiors of the bulbs.

Fueled and enlightened by this (if you'll pardon the wordplay) Tesla felt that the concept of rarefied gas luminescence could be used to light up the night's sky at night. High frequency electric energy could be transmitted into the upper stratosphere via an ionizing beam of ultraviolet radiation. In the stratosphere, gases are at relatively low pressure, like a luminous tube. It would be like the aurora borealis, but generated and controlled by man.

HIGH-FREQUENCY RAILWAY

Tesla's high-frequency railway got power inductively, and discarded the rolling or sliding contacts which were used in conventional third-rail or trolley systems. The oscillating energy was carried by a cable near the pickup bar. Tesla invented this cable to carry these currents, and it remains the precursor of the grounded shielded cable which is used today to carry TV signals and other high-frequency signals. But unlike today's cables, Tesla's high voltage cable used a metal pipe or screen which was broken into shorter lengths than the wave lengths of the current being used. This reduced loss. Since it was required that the shielding not be interrupted, the short sections were made to overlap. yet were insulated from each other.

ELECTRIC FLIGHT

Tesla envisioned electric flight via use of magnifying transmitters, enabling crafts to be go around the world without any need to stop. In 1900, he predicted a cold coal battery that could propel a practical flying machine. This battery would first revolutionize the automotive industry. Tesla is said to have envisioned a personal taxi hovercraft which could be folded and stored like an automobile.

Tesla insisted that power could be supplied without any ground connection. Tesla believed an electromagnetic field existed in the atmosphere. If it could be tapped, fuel-free flight, and at amazing speed, would be possible.

ANTIGRAVITY

Tesla held no patent on any antigravity device, and it's not known if he ever experimented on it, even if he did discuss it at length. This makes him a fixture in UFO reports and other coverage and literature. Researcher/theorist Thomas Bearden, allows for the possibility of gravity control in the physics, which he calls the new Tesla electromagnetic.

FREE-ENERGY RECEIVER

Modern solar panels are expensive. And they are all manufactured by esoteric processes. Tesla's solar panel, on the other hand, is no more than a shiny metal plate coated with an insulating material, which today could be a spray plastic. This panel could serve as an antenna for a capacitor, if the panel were high enough and the capacitor had an earth ground on the other end. Solar energy charges the capacitor through the panel. Adding a switching device to create arhythmic intervals may create electrical output. At night, cosmic rays would continue to charge the capacitor. And this would be free energy, available to anyone anywhere, just as Tesla envisioned.

Tesla's invention surely inspired others in their work toward the common goal of free energy. In 1921 German experimenter Hermann Plauson studied static (electrostatic) electricity, a kind of atmospheric energy which could be readily (if inefficiently) tapped. The aurora borealis reflected this kind of electrostatic electricity.

X-RAYS

Like many of Tesla's innovations, X-rays came from his fundamental belief that everything the human race requires in order to fully understand the universe is actually around us at all times even if mechanical and electronic devices are required to augment our basic understanding of existence.

ELECTRIC MOTOR

Tesla's motor with rotating magnetic fields made possible or vastly improved household appliances, industrial fans, machine tools, disk drives, power tools, water pumps, compressors and electric wristwatches.

LASER

Lasers transformed surgery, and gave rise to most of our new digital media. Everything from George Lucas' Star Wars to Ronald Reagan's Star War Initiative relies upon the laser.

NEON LIGHT

Tesla developed elongated glass tubes which were coated with phosphor and were the precursors of florescent and neon lights. And he discovered that a potentially deadly high voltage current might be rendered harmless by utilizing an alternating current at large frequencies. Tesla predicted it would be commonly engaged for medical purposes.

VERTICAL TAKEOFF AIRCRAFT

Tesla envisioned a vertical take-off and landing aircraft, which combined the features of an airplane and a helicopter. Tesla never built one, but the technology became popular and remains in use to this day. The V-22 Osprey is an excellent example. Tesla likewise envisioned a VTOL with a horizontal turbine, a horseshoe-shaped craft that would ride on a layer of air. Once again, although Tesla never built one of these crafts, a comparable hovercraft is now commercially available.

Traditional method of controlling fluid flow with valves is imperfect due to: mechanical wear of moving parts, inability to control rapid flow "impulses", inability to control the flow when the fluid is highly heated or corrosive. Tesla proposed a fluid diode, an ingenious conduit without any moving parts. Featuring direct vs. reverse current flows, the direct flow is hundreds of times smaller than the reverse flow. It's high reliability and simple construction (no moving parts) made it ideally suited for micro-machines. Medical applications may include drug dispensing in the body.

MAGNIFYING TRANSMITTER

Tesla envisioned a global system of multimedia communication. It was to include planet-wide wireless transmission of pictures, messages, and signals, pictures. Furthermore, he saw this new communication would integrate with extant communications equipment, particularly telephone and telegraph technology.

THE INTERNET

Tesla envisioned an interconnection of all telephone and telegraph lines all over the world, to include the connection of stock-tickers, weather warnings, intelligence transmission, global positioning systems, and energy transmission. He envisioned the interconnection of the existing telegraph/ telephone exchanges or offices in the world; the interconnection and operation of all stock tickers of the world; global weather warning; the establishment of intelligence transmission for exclusive private use; the establishment of secret and secure government telegraph service; the global positioning system.

He submitted a 1902 patent application for The Apparatus for Transmission of Electrical Energy which was finally granted in 1914. J.P. Morgan gave Tesla $150,000 to build the first magnifying transmitter. The Wardenclyffe project was under construction by 1901.

But Marconi was making considerable progress in signal transmission. And with Tesla still wanting to provide the world with free energy, financier J. P. Morgan pulled out of the project. The tower was razed in 1917.

TESLA'S ELECTRIC FUTURE INCLUDED:

• Hydro-electric power generation and of AC for transmission

• Control of atmospheric moisture (which has not yet been accomplished)

• Use in appliances (refrigeration, etc.)

• Lighting, and propulsion use in agriculture

• Microbe elimination and pest control

LITTLE-KNOWN FACTS ABOUT TESLA

• Tesla's rarified circle of friends included writers Mark Twain, Robert Underwood Johnson, and Francis Marion Crawford.

• Tesla discovered X-rays in 1895.

• Tesla tore up a contract with Westinghouse that was worth billions in order to save the company from paying him his huge royalty payments.

• He was an eccentric, driven by what we now call obsessive/compulsive disorder and chronic germ phobia.

• Tesla's idea for a remote-controlled torpedo was rejected by the U.S. Navy. Drones are the current incarnation of Tesla's vision in this instance.

• He began speculating about interplanetary communication, the splitting of the planet Earth, a death ray that could destroy 10,000 planes from over 250 miles away.

• After his death, the custodian of alien property impounded Tesla's trunks. These trunks contained his laboratory notes, his honors, his letters and his personal papers.

• On the 1933 occasion of his 77th birthday, Tesla told reporters that electric power was present everywhere, and in unlimited quantities. He claimed it could fuel the world's machinery, and all without the need of any oil, gas, coal, or other fossil fuels.

- Telsa has been mentioned in tribute by no fewer than three Nobel Prize recipients.

- Tesla was the first to suggest the broadcasting of news and entertainment to the public.

AFTER TESLA

The question of Tesla's legacy is hardly in doubt. His work is everywhere, in almost every device we use throughout the day. Even everyone who uses a GE product or service owes a tip of the hat to Tesla. But who has benefited most? Who most embodies the spirit of Tesla today? Who owes him the greatest debt?

THE HOME COMPUTER REVOLUTION

This is perhaps where the Tesla's contributions are greatest. His work in alternating currents and remote controls made computers possible. He envisioned the internet and also made it possible. So really modern-day geniuses Steve Jobs, Steve Wazniak, and Bill Gates are the torchbearers of Tesla's legacy. And their work has reshaped the modern landscape like no others'.

TESLA MOTORS

Founded in 2003, Tesla Motors not only base their electric cars on the batteries which bear his name. By the close of 2014, Tesla was poised to become the leader in electric automotive manufacturing in the coming decade. Their other interests include clean energy sources which further Tesla's ideas of affordable and renewable energy, widely available and not dependent on fossil fuels. And this is the vision which is most pertinent to our society and to the societies of the future. With global warming on the rise and natural resources on the wane, Tesla's clean energy vision is more valid now than ever. It even seems prophetic. Let's hope it's not too late to heed his call.

CONCLUSION

Nikola Tesla knows how to invent the future, perhaps like no other inventor in history. This very book has been delivered to you through the internet, in one way or another. And the internet virtually saved the entire publishing industry, along with revolutionizing programming broadcast protocols, advertising, and ways too numerous to list. The internet is the future, and it was Nikola Tesla's vision.

And it was a vision realized, like all visions, as a result of one person working on the ideas and discoveries of those who came before. Such is the nature of invention, of science and art and so many of the things which make the human race what it is. In fact, it is invention itself which is the saving grace of the human society, as the creature lacks any natural weaponry or defense mechanism. Our inventiveness became both, and served us well in conquering the planet.

But it took inventors like Tesla to begin looking to save the planet, not conquer it. His clean energy concepts continue to lead the way of our current technological evolution, and in that way he was perhaps as far-seeing an inventor as the world has ever known. Tragically, he was marginalized in his own lifetime and for too long since then. But his place in history is now being restored due to the sheer power of his vision, and its quality and truthfulness and its absolute ability to change the world for the better. Tesla saw power in the Earth, he was the prophet of green energy, and our world without him would be a vasty different, unrecognizable place.

Now you know that, and you know why, and you'll be better equipped to make your own contributions toward inventing the future, which is still exists to be invented. Whatever comes next, it will be bound to the work of Nikola Tesla, his contemporaries and his predecessors, and perhaps take its own place in this vaulted pantheon. The inventors of tomorrow's reality will know Nikola Tesla, because Tesla knows how to invent the future.

EXCERPTS FROM OTHER BLUJESTO PRESS BOOKS

Excerpt from

HARD CELL: How to Use Proteins, Enzymes, Vitamins, Nutrients, Minerals, & Herbs For Superior Health

by Fletcher Rhoden

INTRODUCTION

Why Are Natural Health Resources Necessary For Cellular Health?

Natural health resources, such as naturally occurring proteins, enzymes, vitamins, nutrients and herbals, are necessary to modern healthcare because industrialized healthcare has failed to maintain a healthy population.

The healthcare community agrees that chronic diseases are costs millions of lives and billions of dollars, but it doesn't have to be that way.

Chronic diseases – such as heart disease, stroke, cancer, diabetes, and arthritis – are among the most common, costly, and preventable of all health problems in the U.S. Seven out of ten deaths among Americans each year are from chronic diseases. Heart disease, cancer and stroke account for more than 50% of all deaths each year. In 2005, 133 million Americans – almost one out of every two adults – had at least one chronic illness. About one-fourth of people with chronic conditions have one or more daily activity limitations. Diabetes continues to be the leading cause of kidney failure, non-traumatic lower-extremity amputations, and blindness among adults, aged 20-74. The Robert Wood Johnson Foundation estimates that by 2030, half the U.S. population will have at least one chronic condition.

Chronic diseases came with a price tag in terms of excess direct medical costs, nearly $230 billion over a four-year period that we studied.

Western medicine has done a lot, and the rise of holistic medicine proves there is still a need for much more. The statistics may astound you!

According to CNN one-half of all medical schools now offer courses in holistic health care. Almost one-third of American medical schools-among them Harvard, Yale, John's Hopkins, and Georgetown Universities-now offer coursework in holistic methods. There are five homeopathic hospitals in Great British National Service. One out of three drugs prescribed in Germany is an herb.

The World Health Organization estimates that between 65 to 80 percent of the world's population (about 3 billion people) relied on holistic medicine as their primary form of health care in 2009. In 1993, American consumers spent almost $1.5 billion dollars on herbal remedies-ten times more than was spent on over-the-counter sleeping pills from grocery stores and drug stores.

Approximately $22 million of U.S. government money has already been spent on alternative medical research since 1992 at the National Institutes of Health and Public Health Services.

In 1991, Americans made more visits to unconventional health care providers (425 million) than to conventional doctors (388 million). One out of three Americans were using unconventional medicine in 1991. Americans spent almost $13.7 billion on unconventional health care in 1991. Seventy-five percent of that $13.7 billion (above) was out of pocket.

Twelve percent of Fortune 500 companies offer alternative medicine as part of their health care compensation packages. That percentage was expected to increase to 18 percent by the end of 1996. National Center for Complementary and Alternative Medicine (NCCAM) A nationwide government survey of more than 31,000 adults on their use of complimentary and alternative medicine (CAM) showed that 36 percent of U.S. adults use some form of CAM.

The World Health Organization, estimates that between 65 to 80 percent of the world's population (about 3 billion people) rely on naturopathic or homeopathic medicine as their primary form of health care. Worldwide, only 10 to 30 percent of people use traditional medicine, 70 to 90 percent use naturopathic and homeopathic health care.

Seventy percent of the American population desires a natural approach to health care. Of the one out of three Americans who say they have used natural techniques, 84 percent said they would use it again.

In 2002, Americans made more visits to holistic health care providers (some 600 million a year) than to M.D.s and spend more money out-of-pocket to do so about $30 billion a year by recent estimates.

A lot of this waste has to do with how drugs and supplements are taken. Up until now there have been three choices for nutrient delivery: Ingestion and absorption through the digestive system; absorption through the skin or mucus membranes; intravenously, directly into the blood stream.

Each of these methods has its limitations and drawbacks:

Taking vitamins orally is the most common and least effective. Swallowing vitamins in pill form provides only between 5% and 19% of the total dosage you take into your body; the rest is eliminated by the digestive system. Since nutritional supplements are regulated as food by the FDA, the absorption rate of supplements does not need to be tested, verified or noted on the product package.

Absorption through the skin or mucus membranes works better than swallowing pills, because the nutrients are absorbed directly into the bloodstream. Precise dosing using this method is difficult because of uncontrollable variables.

Intravenous injections, as used in hospitals, work well and dosing is accurate. But administration is difficult, costly and there is a possibility of infection or other problems.

These delivery systems share one major disadvantage. Unfortunately, taking vitamins to optimize nutrient levels may be imprecise at best. In treating sever nutrient deficiencies, and to get nutrient concentrations up to the high levels needed for therapeutic purposes, the dosage levels of vitamins have to be so high that often they cause gastric distress, cramps and diarrhea.

The new liposomal molecular structure corrects these disadvantages. In digestion, our bodies make nutrients available by encapsulating them in liposomes, tiny spherical molecules of lipids, or fat. Once they are absorbed and circulating in the bloodstream, these nutrient molecules fuse directly with the bilayers of cell membranes and the nutritional content they contain is absorbed directly through the cell wall.

LIPOSOMES

One new delivery system of special attention to the holistic community is the Liposome.

Liposomes are an artificially made microscopic drug delivery device consisting of a fatty membrane over a hollow "bubble."

DEFINITION & DESCRIPTION

Liposomes are a wide variety of nanostructures can be utilized as drug delivery vehicles and can be designed and constructed to target specific receptors, to exhibit increased payload and circulatory lifetime by operating in 'stealth-mode', reduce side-effects, improve uptake and efficacy, etc.

Liposomes are structures consisting of one or more concentric spheres of lipid bilayers separated by water or aqueous buffer compartments. Or simply, liposomes are simple microscopic vesicles in which an aqueous volume is entirely enclosed by a membrane composed of lipid bilayers.

USES

Liposomal delivery of nutrients offers a serious advance in nutrient therapy for life-threatening conditions such, but not limited to: Parkinsonism; Alzheimer's disease; autism; multiple sclerosis; congestive heart failure; bi-polar disorder; aging, cancer.

ADVANTAGES

Liposomes provide controlled drug delivery; are biodegradable, biocompatible, flexible; are non ionic; can carry both water and lipid soluble drugs; liposomalized drugs can be stabilized from oxidation; improve protein stabilization; offer controlled hydration; provide sustained release; provide targeted drug delivery or site specific drug delivery; stabilization of entrapped drug from hostile environment; liposomes alter pharmacokinetics and pharmacodynamics of drugs; can be administered through various routes; can incorporate micro and macro molecules; act as a reservoir of drugs, increase therapeutic index of drugs; offer site avoidance therapy; can modulate the distribution of drug; offer direct interaction of the drug with cell."

Drugs delivered via liposomes may be protected from the actions of metabolizing enzymes. Lipophillic drugs may be made soluble. Drugs can be targeted to specific areas by attaching ligands to the liposome. Liposomes are readily absorbed by cells. The rate of drug release may be controlled by the selection of liposome. Using liposomes as a drug deliverer allows potentially lower doses of drug to be used, reducing toxicity and side-effects. Furthermore, it is possible that gene therapy drugs may be delivered by liposomes.

Liposomal drug delivery systems have come of age in recent years, with several liposomal drugs currently in advanced clinical trials or already on the market. It is clear from numerous pre-clinical and clinical studies that drugs, such as antitumor drugs, packaged in liposomes exhibit reduced toxicities, while retaining, or gaining enhanced, efficacy.

Liposomes that allow enhanced drug delivery to disease sites, by virtue of long circulation residence times, are now achieving clinical acceptance. Also at hand are liposomes that promote targeting to particular diseased cells within the disease site. Finally, liposomes are showing particular promise as intracellular delivery systems for proteins/peptides, anti-sense molecules, ribozymes and DNA. The development of liposomes that can be administered systemically and exhibit targeted and fusogenic properties appears to be increasingly within our grasp.

Excerpt from

FIFTY SHADES OF TRAILER PARK BOYS: TPB in the Great Comedic Traditions

By Fletcher Rhoden

Julian, Ricky & Bubbles in the Tradition of Freudian Psychology

Like many comedic heroes, Julian (John Paul Tremblay), Ricky (Robb Wells) and Bubbles (Mike Smith) are everyday men. They're in the working class or lower, relatively uneducated, indulgent of liquor and drugs, sex and pornography and other vices. This puts them squarely in various comedic traditions, but primarily they represent the average person; who struggles to overcome and often fails, despite enough small triumphs to inspire their next efforts. For they always try again, they never back down in the face of adversaries who possess everything they lack; education, money, social graces and haughty attractiveness. From the Three Stooges to Larry the Cable Guy, the struggle of the slobs against the snobs has been and remains a central theme to many comedic traditions.

And TPB is the very epitome of that comedic ethos.

But more than merely being everyday men, they are everyman in another respect; Julian, Ricky and Bubbles collectively present us with a complete human psychological profile. They are three separate parts which combine to make a distinct object separate from the parts. In this case, the whole is nothing other than Dr. Sigmund Freud's model of the human psyche; the ego, the id and the superego.

Freud's model describes the ego, the id and the superego (roughly) this way:

The ego is the component of personality responsible for dealing with reality, governing the impulses of the id, weighing actions and consequences, expressing itself in a manner which is socially acceptable. The ego is reality based.

The id accounts for primitive, instinctive behaviors. The id is driven by the pleasure principle and strives for immediate gratification. The id is impulse based.

The superego is the last to develop among the three in a fully developed psyche. The superego accounts for a sense of right and wrong and presents guidelines for making judgements. The superego is conscience based.

Among the Trailer Park Boys, Julian represents the group's ego. It is Julian who constantly tries to pull Ricky (the id) back from the edges of excess. It is Julian who strives to see the world as it is and to rise to its standards, by one semi-legitimate means or another.

Ricky represents the id. Always wanting to spend whatever cash is on hand, quick to get drunk, buy presents for others and otherwise indulge himself; he is all pleasure principle, the pure id in human form.

Mike Smith's Bubbles is the perfect representation of the superego. Bubbles is the moral center between these two dissimilar criminal types. Bubbles is the only one of the three who is not primarily a professional criminal. He scavenges shopping carts, repairs them and resells them to the same malls he took them from, this is true. But he also offers a service, a craft, and business-to-business delivery. But when Ricky is considering a marital proposal from Barb Lahey (Shelley Thompson), Julian urges against it for practical reasons. She could take half of Ricky's positions if it doesn't work out, Julian explains, and much of that stuff (including a big stash of dope and, ultimately, ownership of the entire trailer park) belongs to Julian and Bubbles as much as to Ricky. The perfect answer of ego to id. But it is Bubbles who adds that one should marry for love, not convenience, and this is the voice of the superego.

In another episode, Ricky is using his daughter Trinity (Jeanna Harrison) and her elementary-school friends to steal barbeques under Canada's Youth Justice Act which prevents children from being sent to adult penal facilities. Julian is frustrated that this will bring unwanted attention to their other criminal activities. But Bubbles is outraged at the moral culpability of Ricky's using children in his dangerous scheme, let alone his own daughter.

In the 2004 Christmas Special, Dear Santa Claus, Go F**K Yourself! Julian, Ricky and Bubbles stand in front of the church before midnight mass. Ricky (the id) is selling grams of hash and marijuana to members of the Sunnyvale community as they pass. He promises that, "The sermon makes a lot more sense if you're stoned!"

Julian snaps at him, "Ricky, you can't sell dope in front of a church on Christmas Eve, it's disrespectful. These are my customers!" Julian is always practical, always dealing with society in a manner that will ensure his survival; always the ego.

And it is Bubbles as the superego who has to explain how morally wrong it is to stand in front of a church on Christmas Eve selling dope.

And consider how these characters interrelate on a more primal level: Id Ricky goes to ego Julian for guidance throughout the series; ego Julian goes to superego Bubbles for guidance; the superego in turn urges ego Julian to control id Ricky. It is a three-way symbiosis in the spirit if not to the letter of Freud's model.

For the id, the governing principle is pleasure; for the ego, it is social expedience; and for the superego, it is moral awareness. In short they are desire, restraint and the morality which results from the one meeting the other. Perhaps in no other modern work of fiction do we see such a clear illustration of this concept than in Trailer Park Boys. A look at how Julian, Ricky and Bubbles fit into the tradition of the comedic trio may shed some light on that subject.

Excerpt from

A PROGRESSIVE CHRISTIAN HANDBOOK: How to Reconcile Your Scientific and Spiritual Beliefs

By Jenni Frendswith

INTRODUCTION

"Render to Caesar the things that are Caesar's and to God the things that are God's." -- Mark 12:17

This is a perfect, poetic description of the new wave of secular and religious thought; progressive Christianity, a new school of Christianity which embraces the secular aspects of the modern world as much as the ancient wisdom of traditional Christian teachings and challenges long-held misconceptions about both. Progressive Christianity embraces the secular disciplines of history and science as well as the spiritual doctrines of scripture and prayer. In this quote, the dual obligations of the individual to the secular and the spiritual seem quite plain, even if society has urged both its secular and religious members to ignore those seemingly opposed but quite naturally interwoven points of view. But after years of unnecessary and in fact dangerous rancor between the secular and the religious communities, our modern and enlightened society has slowly come back to the point at which religion and the secular institutions of government, history and science can once again share the common subconscious; individually and socially. Not only can religion and science once more sit comfortably side by side, they must do so in order to achieve and sustain a healthy social structure. In fact, much of our modern society's ill-health can be directly attributed to the chasm between the religious and secular mindsets, completely without necessity or even advantage.

The cooperation of religion and science is one of the primary concepts behind progressive Christianity; the notion that not only are these concepts not mutually exclusive, but that they are interdependent. Not only is this an intriguing and liberating notion, it is (I believe) the future of both disciplines and of modern society as a whole.

This modest volume will outline the origins and details of this seemingly new social phenomenon and, I hope, enlighten both secularists and religious devotees to a wider and more accurate world view. This broadened perspective should lead to greater mutual respect between the two communities and, thus, a decrease of animus between them. This new affinity could rewrite the way in which we see ourselves, each other, our God and our world and make better things of them all.

This volume will be thorough but not definitive. A variety of examples will be used to illustrate certain points, of course, but a complete evaluation of every such example will be beyond this book's reach or intention. I will outline the precepts and concepts and use biblical passages and examples from modern scientists and scholars, for example, but a complete progressive Christian dissertation on the Old or New Testaments will have to wait for its own volume or set of volumes. Likewise, there is more science in the collected studies of our best minds than can be reviewed here. The introductory nature of this particular volume limits the extent to which I can delve the entire discipline, in fact either discipline.

I will illustrate what this book is and isn't further in the earliest passage of the book, and continue after a brief description of my own history with some rudimentary definitions thereafter; what is secularity? Christianity? What does it mean to be progressive? I'll discuss the Bible and the intermingling of history and myth. I will examine the current definitions of this new term, progressive Christianity, and then redefine it according to political, religious and other social guidelines. This will introduce a brief mention of French philosopher Michele Foucault's system theory and how it applies to modern religious and social perspectives.

Progressive Christianity is, as I said and as I define it, the unity of science and religion in the modern perspective. As such, the history of these two disciplines will be examined, and the progress of their divergence and ultimate re-emergence will be charted. Progressive Christianity also holds that government should remain secular while a person's private life might remain Christian; a separation of Church and State, but not an opposition of Church and State. This subject will also be developed later among the tenants of progressive Christianity.

Progressive Christianity is not only the future of Christianity and of secularism, but a meeting of religious and secular thought that is is the only remedy for the violence which is leading our population into a violent and unnecessary extinction.

BOOK ONE: Conceptual Analysis

What This Book Is:

This book is an outline, a guideline, of a growing social phenomenon; progressive Christianity. As outlined in the introduction, progressive Christianity is the comfortable cohabitation of science and religion (in this case Christianity) in individual and social life. While progressive Christians may differ even on this precise definition, this is my definition and the one which is the focal point of this volume. Some would say that progressive Christianity is simply a modernized Christianity which is more tolerant than traditional Christianity, and it certainly is more tolerant. But to definite it in such broad terms, without taking into account the relationship between religion and science is, for this author, to gloss over the most salient point. It is science that is held in greatest contempt and contention by many religious thinkers, extremists in particular and extremist Christians in even greater particular. So beyond mere social convention, science and its place in progressive Christianity must remain a focal point of discussion. This dissertation is for those people whose world view includes both a spiritual and a secular, and thus scientific, point of view. This book will define the concepts for a newer, more modern world perspective; a more practical, more reasonable perspective. An increase of this shared perspective can only make the world a better, more harmonious and, thus, more godly place. This is a tolerant, fair-minded world view that values the input from both the religious and scientific communities which has begun of its own inertia and the inevitability of its own existence. Modern society could scarcely move forward without this new wave of secular and religious thought; it is the new Manifest Destiny of the human heart and soul.

This perspective, however, includes a new look at some traditional models, including those most revered by the Christian community. A progressive

Christian seeks the meeting of religious and historical disciplines to bring new light to ancient mysteries and to modern complexities.

This modest volume intends to make clear the need and definition of progressive Christianity, its place in history, in the present and in the future. It is a work of analysis, not of invention.

What This Book Is Not:

As said, this book analyzes progressive Christianity, but it doesn't create it. This new wave has already begun, this volume can only introduce it, share it, make it clear to others whose lives can be improved with a wider, more natural world view. But I cannot lay claim to inventing most of its parts, only the sum of the book itself. The concept of progressive Christianity belongs to the hearts and minds of free-thinking and deep-loving souls the world over, whose numbers grow and will, in this author's opinion, continue to grow.

This book is not, as some will claim, a treatise against the concepts of Church and State, nor does it in any way suggest that any government, particularly the United States government, allow religion to unduly influence foreign or domestic courses of action. On the contrary, it is the belief that the State should not be held under any religious sway that is at the very heart of progressive Christianity. If anything, a progressive Christian seeks to reclaim Christianity from the right-wing politicos who have co-opted it to society's great distress.

This book is not an attack on any other religious point of view which might seem to be in conflict with the ones presented here. In point of fact, I believe this particular world view to be the most satisfying for me, but it would not be so if it meant that others couldn't pursue their own beliefs and practices. Much of society's ills, as I will present, are derived from intolerance, and the notion of progressive Christianity (comprised as it is of seemingly opposite viewpoints) is necessarily tolerant of other religious beliefs. And while I do believe progressive Christianity to be the future of Christianity and that a secular and religious viewpoint is destined to be the forefront of the human shared subconscious, I do not claim that this is the only view any person should have. A progressive Christian believes in varied points of view. That, the saying goes, is what makes a horse race.

This book is also not sponsored by any church or corporation or other body other than the author at the time of its initial publication. Later editions by bigger publishers may make this disclaimer outdated at least as it regards corporations. But this is not the thinly veiled agenda of any particular church or other organization, private or public. The personal views expressed are those of the author only.

Excerpt from THE ART OF WAR, THE FIGHT FOR LOVE

PART ONE: LAYING PLANS

1. Sun Tzu said: The art of war is of vital importance to the State.

In War: This seems pretty clear. War is a common occurrence on the geopolitical stage, always has been and probably always will be. It serves several vital functions, including empire expansion and conflict resolution. To master this art form is to stay alive on the world stage, and so it is of vital importance to the State.

In Love When Your Intended is Your Enemy: If you are the State and love is war, your intended may be considered the enemy because he or she must be conquered. And love is certainly of vital importance to you, the State, or you wouldn't be reading this book.

In Love When Third Parties Are Your Enemies: When you have romantic competition, either from rivals or friends or exes, these may be your enemies. The art of war must be practiced on them with skill and cleverness if you are to win the war of love.

2. It is a matter of life and death, a road either to safety or to ruin. Hence it is a subject of inquiry which can on no account be neglected.

In War: Sun Tzu is quite correct to reinforce his first statement by explaining that war is a matter of life death for the state.

In Love When You're Intended is Your Enemy: Love is also a life-or-death matter for modern-day warriors of the heart. A lot of people live their entire lives in loveless misery, or in fear, or at the mercy of smarter, more powerful enemies. And that is a wasted life.

In Love When Third Parties Are Your Enemies: Third-party enemies like usurpers and their minions can bring ruin to your State if you are not careful and if you do not practice the art of war well enough.

3. The art of war, then, is governed by five constant factors, to be taken into account in one's deliberations, when seeking to determine the conditions obtaining in the field.

In War: To be victorious in battle, the general must be deliberate in his actions, and this statement prepares the general to learn the five constant factors to be taken into account in one's deliberations.

In Love When Your Intended is Your Enemy: To be victorious in love, you must understand that the same five constant factors still basically apply.

In Love When Third Parties Are Your Enemies: Whether your enemy is to be conquered (your intended) or vanquished (third parties), you must heed the five constant factors of the battlefield.

4. These are: (1) The Moral Law; (2) Heaven; (3) Earth; (4) The Commander; (5) Method and Discipline.

In War: Any military conflict entails these five factors.

In Love When Your Intended is Your Enemy: Any relationship between you and an intended will involve these five factors.

In Love When Third Parties Are Your Enemies: These five factors can be turned against romantic usurpers or other third parties.

5, 6. The Moral Law

This causes the people to be in complete accord with their ruler and insures the loyalty and obedience of the armies.

In War: When the general has the moral law on his side, he will acquire and retain his people's support and the armies' loyalty. Although a leader without the moral law may still acquire the people's support and the loyalty of the armed forces, he will not be able to retain them, as in the examples of Adolf Hitler or Alexander the Great.

In Love When You're Intended is Your Enemy: When a lover has the Moral Law, he or she will have the support of the people, in this case family, friends and coworkers. This can be crucial, for without this support a lover enters the battlefield virtually alone. Without the advice and guidance of trusted friends and family, conquest on the battlefield of love is very difficult to acquire and, without the moral law, is almost impossible to retain.

In Love When Third Parties Are Your Enemies: When you control the moral law, your enemies will not be able to assail you head-on. They will have to resort to distortion, dishonesty and trickery. These can be powerful strategies, however. Still it is better to hold the moral high ground over them, and to lose the moral grounds to your rivals is to have a severely reduced chance of success.

7. Heaven

Militarily speaking, Heaven includes night and day, the seasons, the weather, cold and heat.

In War: Without taking these things into account, no military strategy can fully succeed. General George Washington's crossing the Delaware, Pharaoh's defeat at the Reed Sea at the hands of Moses; innumerable battles throughout history can be attributed to the clever use of night and day as well as the seasonal considerations.

In Love When You're Intended is Your Enemy: In conflicts of the heart, we may think of these terrestrial conditions in slightly different terms, but only slightly. Are your interludes with your intended daytime occurrences or do they happen primarily at night? Night is more powerful for a seducer, and a clever seducer knows this and uses it to his/her advantage. The season are important too: Holiday seasons have their own rules of romance (many consider the holidays to be an "off-season" for a breakup, for example), and winning or losing the heart of your intended can be reliant upon the seasons. Before you make your move, think about the season; how close are you to Valentine's Day? The Spring often brings vacations; is this something that can be turned to your favor when seducing your intended? In the summer, people are often made irritable from the heat. This may effect your decision to act or to forestall action.

In Love When Third Parties Are Your Enemies: Remember that your enemies will try to use the art of war against you. If you are not mindful of the seasons, the powers of night and day, they will be, and they will use them to destroy you. But you needn't be at their mercy. If you have identified your enemies (your intended's exes, your own exes, new romantic rivals) you will be able to discover how the seasons, the time of day and other aspects of the Heavens, can be turned to your favor. Is your rival making a Valentine's Day advance? Does your competition have a summer physique which you do not possess? Are they spending more nights with your intended, leaving you with the less-powerful day hours? These factors can clue you in to impending danger and help you prepare for it.

8. Earth

Includes distances and topography.

In War: In biblical battles, chariots were often drawn into muddy areas where their speed and agility were countermanded. One of the reasons the United States is so rarely attacked domestically is its geographic location, quite distant from most of its enemies. Israel, on the other hand, must keep distance very much in mind, as it is physically surrounded by its enemies.

In Love When Your Intended is Your Enemy: Is your relationship with your intended a long-distance relationship? This can hurt your chances of success.

In Love When Third Parties Are Your Enemies: Knowing your Earth factors is crucial if you have rivals or usurpers. Whoever has the advantage of proximity, which can vary even in the same city, will have the advantage. More hours of exposure mean greater advantage; so coworkers may be a problem for you; they spend a lot of time with your beloved.

9. The Commander

For Sun Tsu, the Commander must be wise, virtuous, sincere, benevolent, courageous and unyielding.

In War: A successful general or commander uses wisdom, sincerity, benevolence and strictness to win the loyalty and utmost performance of his forces. If he uses them with courage and unyielding dedication and wisdom, his success on the battlefield will be greatly encouraged.

In Love When Your Intended is Your Enemy: If you are the commander in the campaign to win the heart of your intended, you must be sincere and benevolent to win his or her trust and affection. You must be courageous to gain their attention and admiration. You must be wise and unyielding to overcome his or her defenses (doubt, distraction). All of these come into play almost constantly. You must be sincere with your feelings, benevolent to his or her friends and family, courageous against rivals or usurpers. But they also come into play with the very first interaction. It takes courage to ask a man or woman out. It takes wisdom to chose that person well and to approach them in a manner that will inspire a positive response. You must sincerely want to spend some time with that person and convince him or her of that sincerity. And you must be unyielding, lest his or her doubts overturn your courage, wisdom and sincerity.

In Love When Third Parties Are Your Enemies: Here you must be unyielding. Let your rivals know that you are dedicated to defending your conquest against them. Never turn a blind eye to the invasions of an usurper. It will also be wise to be benevolent to them, but only after you have successfully held your ground against them. To charge at their backs will only make you seem petty and will give them a chance for another attack. You do want to be thorough in your vanquishing of this enemy, but don't sacrifice your humanity or you will lose the moral high ground you need for further rule. You must also be wise enough to see your enemy coming, hidden as they will almost certainly be. And you must be virtuous so as to maintain control of the moral law, which in turn will help you maintain the loyalty of your intended.

Excerpt from
SCHOOL XING
A Novel by Fletcher Rhoden

PROLOGUE

My brain is pounding, my skull feels like it's ready to crack. My eyes are aching as they strain to see through the flashing lights. Is this what they all saw, I have to ask myself, all those perps out there who found themselves face-up in the gutter?

Paramedics are looming around me, kneeling and checking my pulse, shouting instructions at each other as they lower the gurney and get ready to slide me onto it. I can barely hear most of them, muttering at each other in their shocked whispers and grim predictions.

The plastic mask fits snugly over my mouth and nose, the sound of my own breathing suddenly louder in my inner ears. Wheezing now, more than I realized.

Not good, I silently note.

It hurts, but my body is flooded with endorphins to numb the pain, which is the only thing keeping me conscious and probably alive.

For now.

The crowd fades in my peripheral vision, the flashing red blotting it out before the ambulance swallows me and one of the paramedics, the doors slamming shut.

Nothing I can do now, I realize, just hold on and pray, if it's not too late for that.

And to wonder.

There was so much more to these events than I was ever privy to. But laying in the ambulance, its siren muffled outside, it's easy for me to see all things more clearly, even things I never saw firsthand.

Hallucinating now? A parting glimpse at the chain of events that's led me here? I can't be sure, can't reason it out; too weak. And that's not what interests me anyway. Not how, not anymore; but what.

And who.

◗

CHAPTER ONE

Only nine days earlier, I wake up the way I always do.

Tired.

But I get out of bed, not because I have a reason, but because I don't have much of a choice. It's either lay here and rot or go somewhere else to do it, and the view of my bedroom ceiling is more than I can stand for another minute. I'm not even willing to try.

The coffee is hot, one of the last simple pleasures. Just a hot cup of Joe, no frills or foam or any of that bullshit. When the hipsters got their hands on coffee, the last bastion of a better world went down for good.

The phone rings, but I let the machine get it.

"Hi, Daddy, it's me. You must be taking a walk; I hope so. I'll try your cell again. I'm just giving you a call to see how you're doing, I haven't heard from you in a while. Stewart and Bobby miss you, Daddy, we wanna have you over to the house for dinner this week. Lemme know what's good. Love you. Bye."

You hope I'm walking? I have to wonder, or that I'm not screening the call? Either way, I love you too, Rachel.

Walking. They'd have me travel five miles a day and go absolutely nowhere, wind up exactly where I started. Thanks, I wanna reply, but I've been doing that my whole life.

I catch a glimpse of myself in the mirror. Gotta take these damn things down, I keep telling myself. I don't need to see the bourbon wrinkles on my increasingly leathery face, bags that have deflated under my eyes to leave permanent pouches, the hair that's much more gray than brown.

I stand up straight, pushing my hair back, wearing the expression I used on so many perps over the years; hardened, angry, intimidating. But the face that stares back at me is old, weak; he knows he's not kidding anyone, not anymore.

Least of all himself.

Maybe you should take that walk after all, I tell myself, get some sun on this clammy skin, some air into these tired, old lungs. But inspiration fades quickly these days, and I'm a lot harder to motivate than I used to be.

I decide to flip on the TV instead, telling myself, I'll exercise my brain for a while; that's pretty much the same thing. Healthy mind, healthy body, isn't that what they say?

Not this morning, they don't.

"... Three people dead reported so far, and at least a dozen injured." The reporter stands in front of an elementary school, I'm not even sure which one. It doesn't matter, I hear myself think. "Police say the gunman, a former student, turned the gun on himself. Reports are still coming in from witnesses to the shooting ... "

Jesus Christ, I think to myself, not again! What's making these people do such things, picking up a gun and roaming through a school, shooting kids and teachers? Why can't we just lock the fucking gates and keep these crazy sons of bitches off the campuses? What is going on with our society that nobody is doing anything about this?

I watch the TV, the screen becoming blurry, a flickering stream of images that I can't focus on. And all I can hear is my own voice ringing inside my head; drowning out the frightened chatter of the surviving students, teachers and faculty.

This can't keep happening! We can't just sit back and do nothing while our kids are being massacred by these nut-jobs. Worse, we're cranking them out every day. This whole world seems like it's designed to drive people crazy, to push them over the edge.

But why do they always land on a school campus? Take your rampage to the Internal Revenue Service or the Senate or whoever else is helping you ruin your life; but leave the kids out of it, for the love of Christ!

My blood starts to quicken; my heart pumping stronger, with greater purpose. My lungs stretch and squeeze; my breath becoming an angry churn, drying my throat and the back of my tongue. My mind is filled with images from my own career: Forty-three years on the job; stacks of reports, countless cups of coffee, innumerable arrests, an impressive conviction rate, a few commendations.

Three kills.

And for what? I have to ask myself, not nearly for the fist time. What was the point?

Take it easy, I tell myself, watch your ticker. You can't look at it that way, you'll be the one who winds up going crazy. Don't forget all the good you did, that the department does; crimes that are prevented, order that doesn't erupt into chaos. Every day that somebody doesn't take a semiautomatic weapon to a schoolyard is a good day, don't forget that.

No, I hear myself thinking. Not good enough, not anymore. That bullshit's fine for getting through the shift, but you can only keep your eyes closed for so long before you realize you're just kidding yourself and everyone around you.

It's pointless and you know it.

The phone rings again, startling me. Christ, Noland, get a grip! I recognize the phone number, of course. This time, I pick up.

"Deac," I say, my voice heavy and low.

"You watchin' it, John?"

"Yeah, Deac, I'm watchin' it."

"Five dead, three of them kids!"

"Five?"

"The count's going up every time I look at the screen. What the fuck is going on out there, John?"

"I was just asking myself the same question, Deac. But I haven't got a goddamned clue."

A sad silence passes. Then Deac's voice, small and metallic coming out of that little speaker in the phone receiver, spits out a jaded sigh. "Fuck it! We're retired, right? Let them sort it out."

I don't answer. It just leaves me cold; a whole lifetime of working so hard to get so little done. Now I can relax and do the same thing thing just by sitting on my ass.

No, I hear that voice say in the back of my mind, where my conscience used to be. No, I can't.

And I won't. Not anymore.

"I gotta go, Deac," I say before setting down the phone, not waiting for a reply. I pull the desk drawer open; my old Beretta 92 in its shoulder holster sitting there, waiting like it always knew I'd be back. I pick it up, the straps dangling over the sides of my wrist. It's heavier than I remember, but it feels good in my hand; formidable.

Deadly.

I haven't worn it since I retired, didn't think I ever would again. I strap on the holster and check the gun. It's clean, loaded and ready.

And so am I.

The shooting took place in Massachusetts, three thousand miles from Los Angeles. But I ain't walkin' any three thousand miles. The Rosewood Avenue Elementary School is only two miles, and I don't even bother with the car. About a mile in I think to myself, See, Rachel? I'm walking!

And I'm lucky to be able to do it, a fact I'm reminded of every time I see Deac. The wheelchair is hard to miss even from two blocks away as he rolls at me, headed toward my place. It's been a long time since Det. Harold Deacons was on the job, or on his feet.

As soon as he gets close enough, Deac stops rolling the chair and holds his arms out at his expanding sides. "John, what the fuck, man? You just hang up on me?"

"Sorry, Deac, wasn't thinking."

"Well, all right, it's cool. I was just worried about you, man. Y'all right?"

"No."

I walk past Deac and he turns the chair to keep pace behind me. "I know what you're going through, John. I feel it too, cuts right through me." I don't answer. But I don't need to. Deac can't walk, but he can still think; and he knows where the elementary school is. "Some reason you're wearing your piece?"

I don't answer. I haven't thought this out, and I'm not sure what I'll come up with once calmer heads begin to prevail. I don't want to be calm now. I've been calm; too calm for too long.

Deac says, "I'm not gonna be hearing about you on tomorrow's news, am I?"

He's only joking, of course. I'm not about to start shooting up any schoolyards. So I don't bother answering him. I haven't got an answer anyway, or an explanation or a plan of action. But I also don't have the brass or the mayor or any of those idiots breathing down my neck. I'm a private citizen now; Det. John Samuel Noland, L.A.P.D.

Retired.

Deac says, "C'mon, John, let's get a beer or something."

"It's not even ten in the morning."

"A coffee then, whatever. Bloody Marys."

"You go."

A few yards later, after pressing on in further silence, Deac asks, "Do you mind telling me where we're going?"

We? I wanna ask.

Yeah, I answer myself in that same doubting moment, we. Deac's the best friend you've got. And he needs you as much as you need him. Don't be an asshole.

So I answer him. "School."

"Well, um, yeah, I kind of got that, John, but ... why? What are we gonna do when we get there?"

This one's not so easy to answer. "Don't know."

And I don't. But it does feel good to be out; to be walking, to be doing something. I look back at the previous half-hour as a blur, a rush of energy that's put me on the street; so strong it's even dragged Deac out of hiding. So at this point I'm pretty much riding that energy, letting it carry me to wherever I'm supposed to be and whatever I'm supposed to do. But how to explain all that to Deac eludes me.

I see the school coming up on my left. It's quiet. The kids are all in class, won't be out for recess for about a half-hour or so. The schoolyard is empty, which always has struck me as vaguely eery; like I can hear the laughter of children who are long gone, grown up and moved on with their lives. This strikes me more and more as I get older, and as these shootings get more frequent.

I can see from the corner that the chain-link gates on the far side of the playground are locked, which is standard protocol. Only the big metal front gate stays open during school hours, which it must do for a variety of reasons.

Deac looks around as we reach the front gate, shaking his head. "See? This is what I'm talkin' about; anybody could walk right in with a machine gun, start shooting up the place, and nobody could do shit about it!"

I look around, thinking more or less the same thing. Deac rolls through the gate, but when I don't he stops and turns. "Aren't we goin' in?"

I give it a little thought. Since I'm really not sure what I'm going to do, I can't really know where we should go. A car drives down Rosewood, a silver Nissan Sentra. Two bluejays chase a crow away from their nest in a plum tree nearby.

"John?"

I stand in front of the school front gate, and I realize what I must do. I've known it all along, I think, without even realizing. My instincts are calling the shots, my brain just a little slow to follow. I warn myself, You'll have to do better than that, Nolan. Too many years sitting on your ass watching television have turned your brain into mush. Look alive, this is important.

Deac looks up from his chair. "So, um, are we just gonna stay here all day?"

"I am."

Deac seems to give it some thought, finally nodding broadly and locking his wheels into place. "Sure, okay, I get it; like we're standing guard."

I'm slow to respond, my brain is already scanning the area on full alert. "Yeah, Deac, standing guard."

"All right, I'm game for that. Let's see any punk-ass perp try'n get by us, right?" After a nervous moment, Deac says, "Hey, shouldn't I have a gun too?"

That isn't a phrase I woke up this morning expecting to hear, and the fact that anyone would be moved to say it in front of an elementary school is tragic.

"This ain't the Alamo," I say with a smile I hope will soften the blow of my remark. "I think you'll be okay."

Excerpt from
THE TRIAL OF DAVY CROCKETT
A Novella by Fletcher Rhoden

Santa Anna's white-gloved slap leapt out in an angry cotton flash. Crockett's bloodied right hand rose up from his side, catching His Excellency's wrist. Crockett pushed Santa Anna's arm back, slamming his hand onto the table. The generalissimo's gold cufflink clattered against the splintered wood with a cracked thud. Blood and dirt smeared on Santa Anna's clean cuff where Crockett held him.

Castrillón's muscles clenched around his tired bones as the two men stared each other down, their mutual tension holding them in a shuddering stillness.

González's saber was already out, Duque's soldados pointing their bayonets at Crockett from five different angles. But this time it was Santa Anna's hand that stayed them from Crockett's final thrust. The fire to kill burned in their scowling eyes, their trembling lips, the veins throbbing on their arms and hands.

"¡Atención soldados, quédense aqui!" Castrillón cried out. The soldados backed away, their bayonets centered on Crockett and Santa Anna, whose hands and eyes were still locked together.

Santa Anna tried to ease his hand away, but Crockett leaned on his wrist, pinning it to the table. "My apologies, Col. Crockett. I swear before God this cursed temper is beyond my control." Crockett looked at him, at first in disbelief and then in distrust. "It is my one great failing," Santa Anna added.

"Next time," Crockett said, "you better kill me." Santa Anna smiled. "On my honor."

Crockett let go and Santa Anna pulled his hand up from the table. González handed His Excellency a clean white handkerchief. Santa Anna wiped his cuff and returned the handkerchief, leaving a disappointed González to step back ignored.

Santa Anna took a purposeful step or two away from Crockett before turning to say, "And what of James Bowie? I understand the great fighter was dead in his cot when my soldados stormed in. Nevertheless, they bayoneted him severely."

Crockett's strength seemed to swell beneath the blood-soaked buckskin.

"It was a tribute, I assure you," His Excellency added, reading Crockett's offense. "Such a man is fearful in death, perhaps even more so than in life."

Crockett's exception seemed to slide away in favor of a nostalgic smile. "Talk about a legend; ol' Jim Bowie actually could wrestle an alligator and put it right to sleep. Hell of a man."

"He was hell in a man," Santa Anna said, "an intoxicated pirate and swindler loyal only to his desires.

¡Falsificador, contrabandista, cazador de fortunas!" Santa Anna spat the words out of his disgusted lips. "And was he any worse than Samuel Houston, whom the Indians call Big Drunk?"

Crockett swayed again, his eyes glazing over as if forgetting Santa Anna's presence, much less his unceasing attack.

Santa Anna added, "Where was the 'Hero of Horseshoe Bend' in your time of crisis?"

Crockett looked as if he was about to speak, but instead lowered his eyelids in a shrewd gambit to withhold whatever information he had.

"He is on the Brazos with that convention," Santa Anna said, "fashioning a government to replace Mexico's and an army to install it. And do not tell me you are unaware of Houston's closeness to our mutual nemesis, Andrew Jackson. Houston, as the representative of the United States president, is a strong force at this committee for a so-called independent Republic of Texas. Do you wonder why, as Jackson's sworn enemy, you were denied aid and left to be slaughtered?"

Crockett winced, either from misunderstanding or disbelief or, Castrillón surmised, an equal measure of both. "Are you saying Jackson and Houston allowed the Alamo to fall just so that a person lowly as me could be killed?"

"You are too modest,Colonel. And were you not insubordinate in holding the mission?" Santa Anna glanced again at Castrillón to add, "Such a crime requires penalty of death."

The words sank into Castrillón's heart like iron balls, sucking the air from his lungs.

"I hear'd Bowie was given discretion and used it," Crockett said. "And far as my enemies are concerned, I was already dead. One man printed I was going to Texas 'to live out my days'." After a chuckle, Crockett added, "I'll never badmouth the press again."

Santa Anna rubbed his right thumb and index finger; the invisible pebble had long since been turned to imaginary dust. "Let us say your band was sacrificed for some strategic gain?"

"I wouldn't know, El Presidente, bein' just a high private an' all."

"Tell me this, if you dare." Santa Anna's words dripped like bile off his tongue. "If your country's beloved George Washington were manning this post, do you think it would have been so readily sacrificed?"

Crockett stared into the gaping truth of His Excellency's observation.

Castrillón considered it too, knowing instantly that every norte with arms to fight would have come to that famed general's aid.

"And you were not dead yet." Santa Anna smiled, more in assault of Crockett than in support. "I heard rumors there would be a President Crockett. That would be the final dagger in Jackson's heart and Van Buren's. Victory here would have placed that dagger firmly in your grip, Colonel."

"They're good men, not mass murderers," Crockett said.

"Where is Fannin, still in Goliad?" Santa Anna's voice rang with familiarity around questions to which he already seemed to know the answer. "Is he cowering in fear of a mere monkey, even with his forces and artillery? Could he not have been ordered to stay off this field until the deed was done?"

Santa Anna stepped back as Crockett tried to push himself out of his chair. His Excellency held one hand out, blocking the soldados' fire upon Crockett as the weakening frontiersman feebly tried to advance.

"Intrigue is the weapon of the powerful, Sr. Crockett. You admitted you came here for political gain; is it not possible those same ends were turned against you?" Crockett strained further, a hissed groan spilling down his chin. "You doomed these men the moment you arrived to fight alongside them!"

Crockett hollered a wordless, blood-filled battle cry. But he was no sooner out of his chair and reaching for Santa Anna then he was falling to the ground, his flattened hands barely halting his collapse.

Santa Anna stood over Crockett, kneeling on the floor .

I should have left him for dead, Castrillón mumbled into his own invisible ear, or killed the poor bastard myself. Those dreams be damned!

But to crush a man's soul, to torture him like this; how can His Excellency thrive on such a -- ?

The hideous truth sank into Castrillón's skull, interrupting his own inner voice.

How can I -- ?

Santa Anna pointed to two of Duque's soldados, each of whom took one of Crockett's arms and set him back in the chair.

Excerpt from

LAST TANGO WITH MARLON

A Novella by Fletcher Rhoden

Wally smiled, gazing into his memory. "Once I was on my way to the set of Hollywood Squares and I came upon this butterfly, a beautiful Lorquin's Admiral. You should have seen it, Bud. I followed that little guy halfway to Nevada, just to see where it was going and to watch it get there. I'm amazed I didn't crash, I barely took my eyes off it for over an hour."

"I'm still amazed you were doing Hollywood Squares."

Wally tossed his hands up, shaking his head. "Everybody knocks Squares. But it's the funniest game show since Groucho's, gets terrific ratings. Saved my ass, I'll tell you that; Paul's too, and a lot of other people's."

"So did penicillin, but I wouldn't wanna sit around watching it on TV."

Wally tapped Marlon on the forearm, guiding him back to the point. "For me, the best things in life didn't come from being on a TV show or a film set, Bud. I may have been content to hawk my jewelry, but at least I didn't take it upon myself to save an entire art form, not to mention a near-extinct race of people."

"They need saving, Wally." The tragedies, the lost lives, the lies and broken promises; Marlon couldn't escape the mountain of horrors. "Governments so corrupt, men so stupid and inept."

"Stupidity, largely misidentified as corruption by the unthinking."

But before Marlon could take offense, Wally added, "And dirty government? That's nobody's idea of a good time. Without the dirty money and the dirty girls and the dirty laughs, what's the point?"

Marlon recognized their dance. They'd always done this, rebut and retort and contradict for the sheer joy of trying to outthink the other. How many parties had they entertained with this conversational counterpoint, Marlon couldn't fathom a guess. But he was getting an idea of how many parties they might have spoiled doing it.

"Look what we're doing to the planet, Wally."

"It's great that you care so much, Bud. But even in the event of all-out nuclear devastation, the planet itself would ultimately recover. It might take millions of years, and Lord knows what would grow here after us; but something would, that's for sure."

"And what about your own race?"

Wally could only sigh. "Have you noticed that the human race is the only race that criticizes the human race? Plus, it's the only race that shows any concern at all for the other races."

"Easy for you to say that, now that you're dead. You think the world'll just take care of itself, that I should stick my head up my ass like everybody else?"

"No, but like so many U. S. presidents, and other world leaders too, I think you're concerning yourself with foreign matters while your domestic front is crumbling."

Marlon rapped his palm against the tabletop and pointed at Wally. "Politics, exactly. What about Vietnam, Watergate? Don't you think those are signs that our civilization is on the brink?"

"As long as we learn from those mistakes. Can you imagine another secluded, elitist, corrupt White House administration like Nixon's, or the U. S. stumbling headlong into another untenable situation like Vietnam?"

There had to be another way to get through to Wally. Marlon picked up the phone. "Hello, Department of Denial? I have someone here you should talk to; he could run your entire western division."

But Wally'd played this little game before. He picked up an imaginary phone that just happened to be sitting right in front of him. "Sir, I'm afraid you've reached the Office of the Obvious and Oblivious. We've got a serious situation here with a man who's trying to solve the world's problems because he can't face the troubles in his own life. Could you hold?"

Marlon grabbed his crotch and said, "Hold this," before hanging up the phone. "I certainly applaud your willingness to take on the bigger opponent."

Wally leapt to his feet and clapped his hands once. Then he pointed out an invisible spectator in a crowd of imagined onlookers. In the looping whine of a turn-of-the-century freak show talker, commonly miscalled a barker, Wally said, "Step right up, ladies and gentlemen, step right up. Come one, come all for a glimpse of the Amazing Marlon; able to take on the mightiest giants and bring the dead back to life. He led a generation of actors out of bondage, folks! He's defied the will of kings and, even more impressively, movie producers. The Amazing Marlon, ladies and gents; he's King David, Jesus, Moses and Elijah all rolled into one!"

"'Aim high,' that's my motto."

Back in his own timid demeanor, Wally said, "Mine was always, 'Walk softly and carry a little twig.'"

"'And hurt a minimum of people.' That's a dangerously old- fashioned outlook."

Wally said, "I was modern enough in my way."

"You were certainly a pioneer of modern therapy. I don't know anybody who kept at it as long as you did; especially considering the effects, or lack thereof."

Excerpt from
WARRIOR TIDE
A novel by Fletcher Rhoden

The Mediterranean Sea: September 26, 1572

The sky was swallowed by storm. Clouds convulsed, dropping rain in heavy sheets and bidding the Mediterranean to rise up and meet them The sea leapt in great walls as if to escape the planet entire, then dropped in crushing frustration for its failure. Watery crevasses of twenty feet or more broke suddenly and alternately, leaving the galley Sol unceasingly on the brink of destruction.

In the cramped companion, the nets barely held the provisions in place. One snap of that chord might send thousands of pounds of cured beef and sacks of oats raining down onto Miguel de Cervantes, leaving him no chance of escape. Outside, the waves crashed against the hull, shaking the galley and nearly blotting the rolling rhythm of the fifty-two oars pulling at full strength. Rodrigo was among those confined to the bowels of the galley, pulling as sun rose and reigned and set again. Now the oars lurched Sol forward as if to outrun the storm herself At least destruction would not come from idleness or surrender, Miguel reasoned, as it surely would to an unmanned vessel in such a storm.

The ropes groaned and twisted as the walls of cured beef and sacks of dried meal leaned out from the walls. Miguel pressed his mangled left hand against the heaving stack of heavy cargo as the Sol listed heavily starboard. Miguel pressed against one crate in the center of a stack of six, his stumped appendage was a fleshy hook; little more than two fingers on half a hand, thumb holding on from sheer tenacity. Infection still plagued the wound, rendering it slow to heal. The swollen purple smelled of shit, but only when the meat would break and drain. It also kept him off the oarsman's bench.

The wound bespoke to all who would inquire everything they would ever know about Miguel de Cervantes de Saavedre; all that would ever be known of him and that enough by ten times.

Miguel had been wounded at Lepanto.

But even his memories of that great occasion, never far from their recent place among his memories, were driven from his mind by concern for Rodrigo and the somber resolve that, if the Lord would have them perish under that inky sea at long last, having cheated the fate so nobly, then it would happen without regard to any futile resistance. Row as he might, Rodrigo would struggle in vein and Miguel would pay the ultimate price for his nostalgia; it would be torn from him along with his life.

With his back in the corner, the muscles of his legs and arms strained as Miguel leaned against the sacks and crates. He closed his eyes, legs pressing the sum of his weight and determination. The waves would push the tonnage behind him without warning, often threatening to toss Miguel across the companion, tumbling into the path of the falling provisions. The unending, staggered cycle of attack and release as the waves tossed the creaking galley drew Miguel's muscles even tighter, each groan of wood a ratchet clicking greater tension in his body until it was as unmoving as stone.

He remained fixed even when the hull tipped so steeply that the starboard wall of the companion was for a long while its floor and Miguel was pinned to its new ceiling by his palms and the desperate soles of his feet.

The hull rolled back and further, to pin him into the lowermost point of the companion; helpless to any falling iron hook or stray musket.

But Miguel remained pinned against the provisions, eyes opening only occasionally to verify his continued existence. The gravity of forces around the galley as she streamed across and sometimes through the waves were only suggested by the cacophony of resistance; wood against water, man against nature, life against death.

The hours crept by in a crashing, churning roll until it ended with more suddenness than Miguel thought possible. Only in the ensuing moments of contemplation could he reason that he'd fallen asleep leaning against the two walls of supplies and that, it the interim, the storm had passed and Sol survived.

His mind set on the dried meats and sacks of meal, several of which had ruptured to spill the fine tan dust of oats over the floor of the companion. It had mixed with the thin layer of salt water that had seeped in during the storm and the result was a thick soup of salty oatmeal, thickening on the walls and in the corners to the delight of the rats who burrowed in and out of the mounds with quickening panic and thirst. Their salty feast would soon cure them from the inside out, but Miguel could not spend even a moment to enjoy their suffering.

He flashed immediately on his younger brother, likely still chained at the bench and expired from exertion or pestilence. Perhaps, in the calm of the storm's passing, there might be time to find Rodrigo and, if the Lord willed it, in such good and healthy spirits as to share his tale of the storm and hear Miguel's own. But the captain could not be allowed to find the companion in such an array, and Miguel stepped away from the netted meats and oats for the first time in uncounted hours. The stiffness in his arms and legs suggested they had been pressing against their charges for no fewer than six hours; the blood that filled his shoes, still sticky between his toes, suggested eight to ten hours. The heat in the companion brought Miguel's attention quickly to the layer of sweat on his forehead and arms, welding his shirt to his back and chest. At nearly a hundred degrees, Miguel knew morning had already matured by several hours and he guessed that it had been nearer to twelve since he'd moved from the corner of the companion.

It seemed an unlikely effort to reach the hand oar Miguel would typically use to disperse the rats and, ultimately, he would never reach it at all. A sudden hum of human voices rose, no words clear in their froth of quick anxiety. Then a crash shook the companion, announcing with the heavy crunch of dying wood and newborn kindling that Sol had been rammed. She lurched again. Outside, the grappling hooks landed with thuds peppering the masts and locking onto the monkey and taffrails before the afferradors finally tied up the forecastle. The rumble of a two hundred feet pounding toward battle gave a tremble to the hull entire, rats darting and cured meats shivering behind the nets.

Always, there were the rats.

Miguel's left hand may have been unfit for the oar, but he could still hold and fire a harquebus; he could still swing a machete or saber if he could find one in the debris of the battle above.

The decks and catwalks were already washed in blood. Miguel could barely see through the clash of sabers and the mist of gunpowder smoke to the Algerian galley that had rammed Sol, lines pulling her into submission. Miguel searched the galley for Rodrigo; his eyes finding the other Algerian galleys as they approached from the port and stern. Beyond them, the rest of the Spanish flotilla was not even on the horizon.

But there were too many Spaniards on Sol's embattled decks for the oarsmen to have been chained, and so turning to liberate an already engaged Rodrigo was no longer a consideration.

Now it was time to fight.

A sickle, used to cut the invader's boarding lines, lay not far from one fallen Spaniard. Miguel pulled him from the deck to remove the obstacle his body might present to his countrymen. His helmet was twice honored as Miguel wore it onto the deck, fixing the Spaniard's dagger in his crippled left hand. The fleshy, festering claw would hold the ten-inch steel blade secure enough to plant it deep into Barbary meat. Miguel only hoped he would have strength enough to pull the knife back out, so as to use it again before his own eventual death.

And it was more than some had; for many it was already a battle of fist against face, fingers against the throat of their enemy. Men pushed their fingers into the eyes of their opponents. Miguel turned to see one Turk smash the ball of his flattened palm into the nose of a Christian only a few feet away. Blood sprang from the Christian's face as his arms went rigid and quivered at his sides.

Flashes of the Janissaries pouring over the decks of the Holy League returned to Miguel's fevered brain. His pulpy hook was once more a hand complete, and once more it exploded as the iron ball passed through it, bone specks jumping out from the wound. But Miguel could allow himself no more nostalgia, however clear the romantic call. Around him, Spaniards were dying; their somber black doublets came alive with broad red splashes of their own blood.

The mace was heavy, solid in his right hand. It swung with a calming familiarity, a favorite weapon since that great engagement under Don Juan de Austria. Now that spiked iron sphere sang a low tone as it cut through the air, bound by chain to the club in his hand and by destiny to the silk-lined skull of his enemy.

Then thunder burst from the traversing gun on the Algerian forecastle, a six-pound ball pushing Sol to a heavy port list as it tore away her poop. Miguel was thrown by the strike, his feet reeling up in front of him as he tumbled backward, the mace falling loose and tumbling across the deck to fall over the monkey rail. His body slid to join it, but Miguel grabbed the mainmast with his free right hand, his left still craned around the ten-inch dagger. His right hand slipped from the wide mast, already slick with blood. Miguel dropped the prized weapon and wrapped both hands around the mast They did not meet on the other side, but his grip was enough to hold him even as several of his mates and enemies toppled past Fewer splashes than men told Miguel that many had managed foot or hand holds on the rails and cheated that water death. Miguel's shoes, little more than seal hide wrapped in twine, slipped against the bloodied, listing deck, but Miguel managed to climb several feet up the mast. From there, at least a better vantage point could be attained.

It brought little good news. Algerians were already pouring in from the second of the four galleys. Miguel recognized the black specks on the horizon as the rest of the Spanish flotilla seemed speeding to the rescue, but one look at the slaughter percolating around him told Miguel that their countrymen would never reach them in time.

Excerpt from
FREEDOM HALL
A novel by Fletcher Rhoden

"But we can't leave everything. We'll fight them off!"

"There's too many," Elijah spat out, his voice swelling with urgency.

Vangie looked around the room in a panic. "But the press, our new leaflet! They"ll burn the house down!"

"Exactly, and we're in the attic, now come on!" Elijah limped to the stairs, Vangie unable to pull herself away. "Vangie, we don't have tome for sentiment. You can always build another house, now hurry up before you get us both killed!" Snorting horses and pounding hooves got louder in the distance, and Vangie turned with a tiny gasp and followed him down the stairs. Gunfire blasted in front of the house, window panes shattering.

Elijah grabbed his .67-caliber smoothbore flintlock pistol from the drawer of an end table at the bottom of the stairs as he limped past. Iron balls whipped unseen through the windows, punching tiny holes into the walls. Vangie ran ducking to the wall of the sitting room, where the Kentucky Plains hung on two gun screws. The crackle of gunfire and the shattering of glass gave her no time to check the rifle, but there was also no need; it was always loaded. Vangie and Elijah were across the kitchen in seconds. Smoke was already thick in the air, rising to announce the flames. As they reached the back door, Vangie could make out the crackle and spit of the fire as it devoured her home.

Elijah grabbed the Kentuck from Vangie and gave her the pistol. "You take this; handles better short range. Don't waste the shot." Elijah lifted the bar lock, pushed open the vertical plank door and peered around to see if they'd been encircled. "Lucky break," he muttered to Vangie. "Let's go."

They ran with their heads low across the back of their lot. Beyond their property line stretched miles of moonlit grassland and swamp. They would have plenty of places to hide of they could get through the open stretch of meadow, but is was three hundred yards with absolutely no cover. Vangie knew it would be a matter of time and luck to determine whether they were spotted and if they would be caught before ducking into the marshland where the raiders' horses and thus the raisers were unlikely to follow.

When Elijah rasped, "Run, Vangie!" she did exactly that, with all her might. Her legs pumped under her and her heart throbbed behind h er ribs.

The ground was firm beneath her feet, it seemed to push her on in her escape. She clutched the pistol to her breast, fingers craned around the oily wood and iron.

When she heard an unfamiliar voice call, "H'yah!" she turned to see how close the raider was. What surprised her was how far away Elijah was. She'd run too fast, she realized, and left him limping behind. He was a cripple because of her and now sheer terror had given her flight to abandon him. He was only fifty yards behind, but the raider was closer to him than that and riding his standardbred at full gallop.

Elijah turned, pulled the Kentuck to his face to aim at the raider, and shot. His tray flashed, muzzle spitting out smoke and lead, but the raider did not go down. His response was to draw his own pistol from his overcoat and slowly take aim. Elijah dropped the Kentuck and ran, his crippled leg propelling him in a staggering gate. He cried out, "Vangie, shoot!"

Vangie looked down at the pistol she just remembered she was holding. She wrapped her fingers around the handle and over the trigger. She raised the gun, but it suddenly felt as if it weighed a thousand pounds. It trembled in her grip, her lungs and heart freezing in the moment to await the outcome.

A gunshot rang out and Elijah fell, his body disappearing in the darkening grass. Vangie screamed and pulled the trigger, the flintlock kicking into her palm with the force of the shot. The raider snapped back but stayed in this saddle, locked in by the stirrups, leaning and bouncing idly as his horse kept galloping forward.

Vangie couldn't move. Her fingers were locked around the handle of the pistol, her legs stiff and arms numb. She'd killed a man, Elijah was dead, and the other raiders were galloping toward her. Her feet sank slowly into the wet ground, the Earth threatening to hold her for capture by her enemies.

Vangie turned and ran for the swamps. Her legs began to flex, pushing her with increasing swiftness away from the men who'd just killed her best friend, cousin and mentor and would surely kill her or worse. She ran without thought, without reason, without the life she'd grown to love. Vangie's memory clanged with the insistent echo of her family's curse. Elijah hadn't become corrupted.

Elijah died young.

Vangie's feet slid and dug into the deepening mud, fast becoming heavier as dirt caked them inches deep and up past her ankles. She lost her left shoe, her run now slightly staggered and much colder.

She ran into marshier terrain with its high grass, soft ground and hidden pools of dark, cold water as the raiders dismounted and searched for her on foot. Her feet were chilled icy cold with the heavy water, seeping into her dress as she squatted down to keep out of sight. The wetness spread across the thirsty cotton until it wrapped her in a thick, wet membrane almost as restrictive as the raiders' proximity and her own terror. At one point Vangie was within fifty feet of one raider, whose line of sight almost fell upon her but for his unfortunate slip on a rock that sent him toppling on his backside. He stood up furious and soiled, waving off the marsh as he led the others back toward their horses.

Once they mounted and started trotting away, Vangie exhaled. An hour later, Vangie stood. her legs were aching and numb and to straighten them took all her effort and inspired considerable pain. But it was nothing compared to the aching of her heart and the hemorrhaging wound in her soul. Vangie wandered back onto the grassland and watched the house she built be consumed in a torrent of orange flame, black smoke and creaking wood.

Vangie stumbled across the grass to Elijah's body, knelt to him and laid his head onto her lap. She rocked him gently and rubbed his cold, blood-caked cheeks and chin. Her breath became a churning wind of sadness and loss.

She'd never see him again, she realized. they'd never spend another night bantering and laughing and crafting words each hoped would reach out and change their world. She'd never see that vaguely confusing look on his face that would come and go so quickly; her heart would never flutter upon its discovery. They would never bump heads on the method or manner of their prose; he would never prover her wrong, no she him. He'd brought her life and she brought him death. The last of his blood was warm but cooling fast, soaking into her dress and dripping down her thighs.

Elijah was dead, she reaped to herself, the notion of her isolation flooding her swollen heart. She squeezed him tighter, fingers digging into his chest; he didn't flinch. She cried until her throat was as fleshy and red as his scalp.

The pounding emptiness of her vacant soul told her beyond denial that she did love Elijah, more than she'd allowed herself to admit. Now the truth of Carroll's insight was beyond doubt. She did love h im and she was in love with him, a passion never to be consummated. Every shred of hope, itself a burden, fled to leave her in even greater anguish. It bent her frown, lips peeling up and over her teeth to give way to her gushing sorrow. Her brows cramped, her forehead creasing to comprehend his loss.

She loved him. She loved him so much.

And now he was dead.

Her heart strained to keep beating, tackled by a seething, prickling torture. Vangie thought about her mother and Sarah. She thought about her father, probably alive down in South Carolina; that he didn't deserve to live on the Earth that the good and noble Elijah was denied. It was her father's act of pushing out the window that gave him the limp. But Vangie's mind immediately took the next step, as it always did when she tried to blame her father or anyone but herself for h er misfortune. She lied, purposefully inciting him, and the results of her gamble would send Elijah falling to break his leg on the gravel roundabout.

She was at fault. If she'd left the attic when Elijah told her to, or shot the raider a few seconds sooner; if she hadn't been so consumed with fear and actually had some of that courage and determination, Elijah would be alive.

Vangie tried to reassure herself that life was short and that even the greatest of men have to leave it eventually. But that reassurance didn't make his loss any easier.

Please don't be dead, Vangie's heart cried without air to support its miserable plea. I'll undo whatever I did, I won't be whatever I was if you'll only come back and end this nightmare.

Please come back, my love.

Vangie lowered her face over Elijah's, knowing the only comfort she could bring would be to herself in hiding from the judgment of God. She couldn't show Him her face, or the society or perhaps anyone, should she be so lucky to have that chance. And it would be luck, for Vangie was certain she wasn't deserving of it.

Elijah was dead. And it was her fault.

She'd sacrificed the privilege of service; in her trembling hands she held the proof of its futility, the guarantee of her failure. Vangie vowed that she'd never put anyone in the dangerous proximity of her incompetence again. The world would have to fight for itself, the cause would have a better chance without her blundering.

The life she'd lead now stretched out in a vacuous tunnel of echoing sorrow and loneliness. In her mind, she was already walking.

Excerpt from
NEVER DIE TWICE
A Novel by Fletcher Rhoden

Jonathan was starting to feel lose; an easy chuckle finding his lips, his knee touching Bethany's as he raised his second glass.

"After my mom died, I guess I was just glad to get outta Barstow." Bethany took another sip. "Now I'd just like to get outta Laughlin."

Her skin was smooth, freckles scattered across her creamy cheeks. Her fingertips were cool as they drew invisible lines along his forearm. Her fragrance was delicate, a pretty vapor veil drawing Jonathan closer. Flashes of Trish filled his memory with the hours at the top of Mulholland; the sticky palms, car windows fogged, the gentle force of her face pushing against his.

"Having a cocktail, Jack?" Jonathan turned as Victor strode up to them. He was smiling, even if his parental sternness was easy to detect under the surface. Victor nodded to Bethany and said, "Delighted to see you again, Miss Bethany. But were you aware that this young man is only -- ?"

"On a ten-minute break," Jonathan interrupted. "We were looking for something . I really should be getting back to work." Jonathan rose under Victor's supervision, turning to his frowning grandfather. "Let me get the check and we'll to take care of that, that thing we have to, uh, to take care of."

Victor tossed a twenty dollar bill on the table and said, "I insist," before turning to Jonathan and adding, "shall we?"

Jonathan turned to Bethany. "I'll see you again, for dinner?"

"Sure."

Victor's stride was particularly quick, and Jonathan had to walk faster than normal to keep from being trampled by a man in his seventies.

"Look, I know you're a little pissed that I had a drink. Right, two drinks, but I only finished one. Anyway, I've had a gin and tonic before, it's no big deal. I mean, no kid could be as innocent as my father wants to think I am, even though I'm sorry to say I come pretty close."

Without turning to face Jonathan, Victor assumed the lead, stepping ahead to take them past the inlet with the elevators.

"But no, you're right," Jonathan went on, "I need to be on my toes. The mission is what's important. I guess I was thinking, y'know, the whole shaken-not-stirred thing, wooing the pretty girl, sipping a cocktail. I know people used to drink more then than they do now, but it's still part of the ritual, right, part of the game?"

They arrived at a door marked stairs and Victor pushed it open, Jonathan staying close behind him. "Hey, where are we going?"

The plush dark of the hotel lobby gave way to the vacuous cold of the staircase; metal stairs catching every sound to bounce from one concrete wall to another.

But the change of scenery was nothing compared to the change that had overtaken Victor. "What's wrong with the elevator?" Jonathan asked his newly sullen grandfather. Then a hopeful crackle warmed Jonathan's brain. "Is this one of the secret entrances to the underground lair?"

Victor stood in a paralyzed rage until the door clicked shut behind Jonathan. Then he turned and rushed at Jonathan with that wide, thick frame. Beyond Jonathan's shock to be suddenly under the old man's attack, he was surprised at Victor's quickness, the power of his left forearm as it pressed against Jonathan's upper chest and forced him against the wall.

Victor pressed his face near to Jonathan's, those old blue eyes burning with anger, lips pulled tight over his false teeth. "You called them."

Jonathan's mind raced, his tongue stumbled in to buy him more time. "What?" Jonathan feebly offered. "Who? What are you -- ?"

"Don't try to con me, boy! You called your parents, your cohorts in crime. You've been in league with them ever since we left Los Angeles!"

Good, go ahead and think that, Jonathan said in his imagined voice. I'm the freakin' Captivus and you've solved the mystery, okay? Now let's go home!

But it would never work, Jonathan knew instantly, seeing instead the image of his grandfather rushing off alone. One step into a trucker's cab or Greyhound bus and he'd be impossible to find. He'd die out on his own, and it would be Jonathan's fault.

"XL, it's not true," Jonathan said.

"Liar!" Victor pulled Jonathan's Nextel Motorola 190C out of his pocket, a quick cold stone sinking into Jonathan's belly as he slapped his own trouser pockets, finding them flat. "Your father called for you," Victor said, "let it slip that you called him last night, ready to negotiate. Trying to make a better deal for yourself before turning me over to Captivus? No wonder you were so ready to come on this mission! You were leading me into a trap!"

"But I wasn't eager to come here," Jonathan said, his words fast and desperate. "You had to convince me, cajole me, even threaten me."

"You people are pathetic. If your parentbots were his first line of attack and you're his secret weapon, Captivus hasn't got a chance."

"You got it all wrong, XL. I mean, yeah, I did call them, that's true; last night, like he said. But you said I should. Don't you remember talking about it back in Barstow? It was your idea, as I recall."

Victor's eyes were shrewd slits. "Last night I asked what you'd done, you said you'd only bought the toiletries. Why did you lie?"

Jonathan tried to ignore his racing heart, his dry mouth and rubbery tongue. "I thought you meant, 'What else did you buy?' So, I said, 'No, I just got the stuff.' Y'know, as opposed to getting other stuff; like a cocktail or whatever."

"A lie is a lie, Jack."

Jonathan nodded, noting the slightest softening of Victor's tone. "Yes, you're right, absolutely, XL, I did purposefully leave the call out of my report. I guess I wanted to... I was trying to run things on my own a little bit. I wanna be the kind of agent who takes the initiative, who leads, controls the situation; like you, XL."

Victor's eyes remained guarded slits. His forearm relaxed its position against Jonathan's chest, lowering as Victor eased backward without actually taking a step. "So, what kind of game were you running, then?"

"Well, uh, I knew the folks would report back to Captivus. Now, I told them we were in Las Vegas -- "

"You told them that? Why?"

"To throw 'em off the scent, like we discussed back in Barstow." The truth mingled with the lie to form a smooth concoction, rolling with greater fluidity off Jonathan's squirming tongue. "But when they go back to Captivus with this information, they'll be wrong, and that'll disenfranchise them from him."

Victor finally stepped back, Jonathan straightening his own tuxedo jacket.

"And with your folks on the outs with Captivus, they might turn coat and help us in the clutch, even unknowingly. Good work, Jack."

Jonathan took a deep breath, the oxygen fresh in his lungs. "One thing," Victor said, setting Jonathan's heart skipping again. "I don't like surprises, boy; there'll be no more going out on your own." Victor's voice was stern again, but it no longer clapped angrily against the walls to echo in the tall, cold chamber.

"From now on we tell each other everything," Victor went on. "Our lives depend on one another, lad, and we have to be able to trust each other, to believe in each other completely."

About the Author

In addition to being a popular author, Fletcher Rhoden is also a produced playwright (Soul Cancer, Last Tango With Marlon, Redhead Cuban Hausfrau Husband). The Los Angeles native is a popular lecturer (The Art of War, the Fight for Love: the Workshop; Fifty Shades of Trailer Park Boys: An Evening with Fletcher Rhoden; Write Makes Might: Stronger Structure in Storytelling), solo-exhibition painter and muralist (Fletcher Rhoden Sleeps with the Fishes, 2007), produced film writer (Stump the Band, Boathouse Studios, 2007), creator of animated short subjects (Spike & Mike's Sick & Twisted Festival of Animation), accomplished musician and composer of over 500 songs with several music CDs & DVDs available online.

www.fletcherrhoden.com

www.ingramcontent.com/pod-product-compliance
Lightning Source LLC
Chambersburg PA
CBHW070650290526
45790CB00001B/262